Gone SWIMMING

A Guide to Embracing Singleness
and Achieving Adulthood in Christ

TATIANA A. HARRIS

ISBN 978-1-7364888-0-5

Editing, cover design, and formatting by ChristianEditingServices.com

Author photo by Ricardo Metayer

Printed in the United States of America

Disclaimer

Gone Swimming is for everyone and anyone to simply enjoy and learn from of their own will and desire. At the time of this publishing, I am currently a Registered Marriage and Family Therapy Intern in the local community. However, I wrote this book simply as a woman who has personally experienced her own season of singleness, not as a clinician. Please be advised, the content of this book is *not* to be seen, or steps taken by the reader, as professional therapeutic counseling. If you feel you need professional counseling, I urge you to seek services from a licensed therapist. *Gone Swimming* is a spiritual self-help book I felt compelled by God to write prior to becoming a clinician. This book unveils one aspect of my many transformative experiences as an individual.

Although my faith influences my approach as a professional, my faith does not discriminate against those of other faith views. The details of this book are solely my personal experiences, shared to illustrate the life lessons I have learned thus far in my own spiritual journey. The guides included throughout the text are for those seeking to obtain an aspect of spiritual guidance *apart from* and *outside* the realms of therapeutic advisory or recommendations.

Prioritizing due diligence to the client as well as client autonomy are two of the many ethical codes I consciously implement as a growing clinician. In addition to the state laws I am currently practicing under, I also adhere to the American Association for Marriage and Family Therapy (AAMFT) Code of Ethics. If you are in crisis, please seek mental health services by researching a local clinic or nearby hospital or by searching online for therapists in your community. In case of an emergency please contact 911 or the National Suicide Prevention Hotline at 1–800–273–8255 or visit their website, https://suicidepreventionlifeline.org.

Acknowledgements

Thank you to my parents, Drexel L. Harris and Ingrid N. Harris, for raising me, loving me, and believing in my dreams.

Teach a child in the way they should go and even when they are old, they will not turn from it.

—Proverbs 22:6

Table of Contents

Introduction

Imagine yourself in a pool.
This pool is your current life.
This life is *singlehood.*

A few years ago early one cold morning in Gainesville, Florida, I was walking to the bus stop, heading to campus, when I felt as though the Holy Spirit tapped me on the shoulder and asked, "Why are you choosing to stay in the pool when I'm preparing you for the ocean?"

To be honest, at first I wasn't entirely sure what the question even meant, let alone aware of where it was coming from. As I continued walking, I began to consider the collective years of my existence. At that time, I was twenty years old and, to my shame, realized that God was right. Why was I staying in the pool instead of following Him to the ocean?

For a long time I had been fully aware of what my mind-set was and how I was choosing to live, but completely avoiding examining those decisions. Unfortunately, this avoidance was hindering my ability to enjoy life for what it should be: a full life with Christ. Why? Because I was so distracted by what I wanted it to be: filled with another individual. I was clinging to the pool's ledges for dear life.

Now let's back up. What is all this talk of pools, oceans, and ledges anyway? Well, with time and through much prayer, God started to make very clear to me the true picture of my existence at that particular time in my life. The parallel here is that my singlehood was "the pool." I was in it but not allowing my mind to consider that. And "the ledges" were the various guys in my life "pool" whom I spent most of my time clinging to. Starting to get the picture here?

I asked myself why I had been clinging to pool ledges for as long as I could remember, and why God was *now* questioning me about my preference to stay in the pool. This book shares the answers to all my spiraling questions, which—if you are or were single— you've asked yourself in one way or another at some point. My hope is that sharing my personal experiences will enable you to examine your pool and grow as I have in the wonderful stage called singlehood.

The beauty of this "stage" is just that—a temporary span of time that can change at any point. However, marriage is not *promised,* and there is nothing wrong with deciding to remain single. We must keep in mind, especially as young adults striving to live for Christ, that God (as our good and nurturing Father) decides when we're ready to move from one stage of life to the next, and He determines the nature of those stages in accordance with His perfect will.

Being completely honest, I had shamefully gotten myself into countless bad situations with multiple guys over the span of my late teens and early twenties. I thought I cared a lot for each of them when, in reality, it was my own selfishness and desire to be in control that I thought would force me out of this stage. The result? Holding myself hostage in singlehood for much longer than I, and God, desired. Thereby His question to me, "Why are you choosing to stay in the pool when I'm preparing you for the ocean?"

In hindsight, I see now that this extended time of singlehood was ultimately for God's glory and my growth. I'm sure of this, not only because I'm able to openly share my testimony with you but also because of the overwhelming amount of *grace* I continued to receive from Him during that time. This truth resonates from Romans 8:28:

> In all things God works for the good of those who love him, who have been called according to his purpose.

Since the very day I got baptized and made Jesus the Lord of my life—September 10, 2006—I have read the following verse just about every night before going to sleep:

> If you believe, you will receive whatever you ask for in prayer.
>
> —Matthew 21:22

Like most young people moving through the teen and early-adult years, though, I kept changing the things I was praying to receive— as often as every few months or so. As teens and young adults, most of us have prayed for something but found the prayer continued to change over time in our Christian walk, whether about a relationship, school, job, career, a weight goal—you name it. I believe the reason my prayers for a person or thing kept changing, if I'm being honest, is that I didn't focus on the first part of that verse: "If you believe."

I did not believe.

Because I did not believe, I could not *trust* God.

Looking back, I see that throughout most of my singlehood I didn't trust in Him to answer many of my prayers, especially for Him to bless me with what I thought I needed most: a relationship.

This is the confidence we have in approaching God:

that if we ask anything according to his will, he hears us. And if we know that he hears us—whatever we ask—we know that we have what we asked of him.

—1 John 5:14–15

All these people were still living by faith when they died. They did not receive the things promised; they only saw them and welcomed them from a distance, admitting that they were foreigners and strangers on earth.

—Hebrews 11:13

I want it to be evident at my death that I lived by faith through every life stage.

While sharing my personal story with you, I've included thought provoking, Scripture-based questions at the end of each chapter, with space for you to write your personal reflections and describe how you'll go about implementing change in your spiritual life. I've titled these application sections "Walk with Me," with the intention and hope that you'll not simply read but also apply in your heart and life all you're taking in.

> Applying healthy changes to our spiritual lives evokes healthy changes in everything we think and do.

I hope you enjoy this testimony and workbook. Feel free to write, underline, draw, and highlight on any page—even in the margins. Grab a nice cup of coffee, tea, or hot chocolate and your colored pens and highlighters, get comfortable, and dig in. In my opinion, the best part of learning is found in the unexpected epiphanies as lessons begin to make sense, so I urge you to take note of those aha moments.

CHAPTER 1

Are You Talking to Me?

Identifying Yourself and Your Struggles

In my desire to control my own life rather than trusting God to lead me to His best in all things, I figured I could avoid being in deep water (simply accepting that I was single) by clinging to the ledges of my pool and hopping out as soon as I found a ledge that would help get me out.

> Only when we realize who we are and identify the weaknesses in our character are we able to begin working to correct them.

My original intention was for a guy to help me out of the pool of singlehood, but none of the guys I developed feelings for were a help. Still, I clung to those ledges.

Oftentimes, instead of learning and working on being simply a good friend, I found myself being needy, clingy, and frustrated to the point of tears. Honestly, I was outright annoying. Even though I couldn't get myself into a relationship, I grew comfortable with the stress I was causing myself and the male friend instead of enjoying our friendship while also spending time on my own. In a selfish, needy state of mind, the unnecessary stress seemed better than boredom and being at home alone. Has there ever been a time when you felt that way?

After years of behaving in that constant emotionally destructive state of mind I'd developed by choosing not to understand the *role* of singleness in my life, I had to question myself: *How can this irrational mind-set of fear and discontentment possibly be pleasing to God?* The answer came so clearly that it was blinding at first. The reality was that my behaviors were *not* pleasing to God. Although I had known deep down that continuing this unhealthy lifestyle was not pleasing to Him at all, it wasn't until I was much older, physically and spiritually, that I started making real long-lasting changes.

Writing this book over the course of a few years was a significant part of the transformation I'm sharing with you. The process took much time. Why, you may ask? Well, because when you spend much time living a certain way, you're planting seeds whether you realize it or not, and eventually there will be a harvest. Unfortunately, I was not pleased with my harvest. I reaped bad thoughts and poor actions. Therefore, before I could start planting new seeds (implementing my changed mind-set) I had to *uproot* what I had allowed to grow for far too long. This realization came to life for me when I read Galatians 6:8 (TPT):

> The harvest you reap reveals the seed that was planted.

In my early twenties I could finally see how much God was caring for me and investing in me and had been all along. I finally recognized that I had been rejecting the seeds from His Word and accepting and planting the seeds of this world: the seed of discontentment, the seed of pleasure, the seed of selfishness, the seed of deceit, the seed of "woe is me," and the seed of "when is it my turn, Jesus?"

What happens when you place a seed in the ground and give it water and sunlight? It grows. I was watering my worldly seeds with the tears falling from my eyes because I was refusing to take the focus off myself and instead focus on the cross of Jesus.

As disciples of Christ—true followers—we must genuinely understand this reality: Our lives are truly not our own but under the Fatherly care of our Creator, God, who understands what we need and when we need it. He alone provides for us the right seeds in due time. Imagine giving a child a seed to plant in the backyard or a small garden at school and months later the child comes back to you with a completely different plant than the seed you had given them? What would you say to the child? And imagine their response to you! "Oh, I didn't like the kind of seed you gave me, so I traded it for a different kind." So ridiculous, right? Who trades a seed? A seed is too small to even know what it's going to become, let alone understand its full value. For us to view God in this way— deciding we're going to trade what He's given us for something else—comes from a heart known as *ingratitude.*

> We must remember that we are here not only to be cared for by our heavenly Father but also to listen to Him and obey Him.

He has made everything beautiful in its time.

—Ecclesiastes 3:11

Society, institutions, establishments, political parties, schools, sports teams, Hollywood, and the like all want to mislead us to believe that our lives are to be experienced and lived only for *self.* However, as new and transformed creations by salvation through Jesus Christ, it is our responsibility to remember this truth: the world's point of view is the furthest thing from truth.

As I approached my early twenties, my ledges started pushing me off—more like shrugging me off if I'm being honest here.

Realizing this truth, I understood exactly why the Holy Spirit had chosen that time in my life to ask me why I was "choosing to stay in the pool." He was calling me to find the courage to overcome my discontentment and then help others overcome theirs. I also realized my life had always been about *me* rather than about the One who created me, who planted a distinctive purpose in me. He is a good, nurturing Father who desires to care for me in His divinely best ways. Every decision I had made, every fear in me that I had allowed to grow into full bloom, every dream I had written in my quiet-time journal all pointed to the same self-centered person: me.

When we're displeased with our inwardly focused realities, how often do we choose to create alternate ones in our heads in search of lasting peace and contentment? Can you relate? How often have these short-term alternate realities failed us, ultimately leaving us more displeased than we had been in the first place? Every time.

Take a moment to ask yourself this: Am I willing to surrender to Jesus and be used by God in *any way* He pleases, trusting that He *is* my good, nurturing Father with a perfect plan?

Write your honest initial response:

_____

_____

_____

_____

_____

_____

As you continue reading, it's important to keep in mind that we were each placed on this earth for a specific God purpose. Often we go through circumstances for the additional purpose of being equipped to help someone else. Isn't that crazy—to consider a trial or tribulation you've gone through, may have even experienced for years, has prepared you to help someone who is going through something similar? Think about what Christ did for us. He suffered and died that we might have abundant life and eternal life in Him and share that good news with others.

> I have come that they may have life, and have it to the full.
>
> —John 10:10

If we want to live lives as true followers of Christ, why are we quick to forget to follow Him? Or do we deliberately choose not to follow His excellent example of being a living sacrifice? In your life, in this moment right now, can you honestly say, "I am a living sacrifice"?

I've had to ask myself the same question many times throughout my walk with God, only to find time and time again that my answer was no.

I mentioned earlier that I would share parts of my personal story in hope that you will take something away from my past learning experiences. I want to take you back to a specific time in my walk with God when I knew for a fact that I was not practicing Christ's model of a living sacrifice. I was a freshman in undergraduate school, attending the University of Florida, and I was eager for what awaited me because I'd moved away from home for the first time. I was excited to be somewhere completely new. For as long as I could remember, I couldn't wait to grow up, find my true love, and get married. Almost every young high school graduate's dream, right? Right. Okay, glad we're on the same page here.

Unfortunately, instead of being entirely focused on how I could be used by God, I was more concerned with how I could *use* my relationship with God for myself. To my dismay, this way of thinking completely messed me up spiritually, mentally, and emotionally. My lack of contentment in my young-adult stage of singlehood prevented me from falling even more in love with God. It prevented me from appreciating deep relationships and bonds with sisters (young women my age in my campus ministry) and even from being grateful for spiritual relationships with brothers (young men my age who were believers and interested in platonic friendships). Being transparent, for most of this time I allowed my selfish desires to reign over my life, completely taking myself away from what God had set up so beautifully for my stage of singleness. I began to see the negative impacts this unwanted harvest was causing in my life, but I didn't know how to break my spiraling, emotionally driven cycles.

> Selfishness can cause us to lose our internal spiritual compasses and ultimately wander away from God in our hearts.

A very special person served as a significant part in the process that opened my eyes to the error of my ways. As I shared earlier, my heart and mind in high school and college were not focused on the right person (God) or on the right relationship (with Him). Even though I was a believer and participating in a campus ministry, I allowed my self-centeredness to distract me from following God's instructions wholeheartedly. To make a long story short, right away I liked a brother and decided (in my mind) that one, he was going to be my boyfriend; two, we'd date after being friends for a year (because I wanted to make sure we were actually friends first, duh); and three, we'd get married right around the time I expected to graduate. Sounds like a beautiful plan, right? Wrong. This bright idea almost ruined my life. Literally. What should have been a simple brother-sister relationship or light crush turned into a journey of confusion, heartbreak, and eventually sin because I refused to let go of my own desires in order to take on God's plans for me.

Over the course of four years, I continued to allow my emotions to be swept from one young man to the next while still hoping my dream would come true to be with that first brother I had wanted to date. My refusal to repent got so bad that he approached me and said, "Tatiana, I feel like we've had this conversation before"— meaning he was being very clear about his intention. He had no plans to pursue me, but I was not accepting his refusal.

So why am I sharing this? The answer brings us back to the purpose of this book: a guide to *embracing* singleness—a healthy acceptance that is required in order to thrive through the stage of singlehood. I was not thriving.

There were, however, periods of time during college that I genuinely enjoyed being single. At times I thought I had truly accepted that stage of my life, only to realize that if I had really changed I would not be repeatedly going back to my old habits, trying to take my life into my own hands again. I can honestly say that those periods of accepting singlehood were beautiful and what I now acknowledge as *contentment*.

During those contented times, I was able to study the Bible with many young ladies I had met on campus, help plan and serve at different campus events, lead group Bible discussions, attend conferences, excel in my classes, and grow in my knowledge of God's Word. Even so, as God made attempt after attempt to fill me up and make me whole, I'd eventually reject His favor and choose discontentment again.

I recall how I felt after a particularly full day of serving and encouraging others. I felt poured out like a drink offering. By the time I arrived home, I felt so lonely that I lay in bed and cried myself to sleep. I'm sure you can (or will at some point) relate to this feeling, right? Unfortunately, I was not allowing God to enter the deepest parts of my heart because I was still waiting to be filled with something else or by someone else.

Why is it that moments of contentment are temporary? We'll touch on this topic again later, but here's the cheat-sheet answer for you now: Satan. His full intent is to distract, discourage, and disrupt. The Bible refers to him as "the thief" in John 10:10. He "comes only to steal and kill and destroy." As I shared earlier, the second half of this verse addresses God's role in stark contrast: "I have come that they may have life, and have it to the full."

> God's desire through His Son, Jesus Christ, is for us to experience life to the *full*.

Looking back at that time in my life, I realize that my definition of a "full" life did not coincide with God's definition.

Four years later I graduated from the University of Florida and moved from Gainesville. In so many words, I left my long-term interest behind in my first attempt to reach out for God's already outstretched hand. Perhaps you've been there too, where you felt so deeply for a person and couldn't understand why God would "allow" you to have those feelings if they were not meant to be reciprocated. Well, I'm here to tell you that it's not a matter of God "allowing" you to have those feelings but rather a matter of your own choice in how you exercise free will.

We each have the freedom of choice to either love God above all else and all others or to love ourselves and others above Him. This may sound harsh, but understand that this truth comes from God's Word, from a place of authentic love, and with a hard warning. At some point, even when we have no idea where God's path may lead, we each have to decide if we're going to let go of self and let God direct our paths or continue to turn from His immeasurable favor, love, direction, and guidance. He doesn't force us but warns that until we turn to Him through Christ, His Holy Spirit will not move in and through us because we have not chosen to make *room for Him* as Lord of our lives. Jesus said,

> "I am the true vine, and my Father is the gardener. He cuts off every branch in me that bears no fruit, while every branch that does bear fruit he prunes so that it will be even more fruitful. You are already clean because of the word I have spoken to you. Remain in me, as I also remain in you. No branch can bear fruit by itself; it must remain in the vine. Neither can you bear fruit unless you remain in me.
>
> "I am the vine; you are the branches. If you remain in me and I in you, you will bear much fruit; apart from me you can do nothing. . . .
>
> "As the Father has loved me, so have I loved you. Now remain in my love. If you keep my commands, you will remain in my love, just as I have kept my Father's commands and remain in his love. I have told you this so that my joy may be in you and that your joy may be complete."
>
> —John 15:1–5, 9–11

God is always *able;* the problem is that we are not always *willing.*

This brings us back to lack of trust. Sometimes we're unwilling to obey because we don't trust God. I encourage you to overcome your fear that is preventing you from plunging into the pool of singleness wholeheartedly. I encourage you to embrace His love already given to you through Christ Jesus.

> Trust in the Lord with all your heart and lean not on your own understanding; in all your ways submit to him, and he will make your paths straight.

—Proverbs 3:5–6

Denial of self-worth and God's love results in even deeper despair, but the good news is that there are ways to overcome the cycles and become steadfast in faith. The first part of this process is *repentance.*

Here are five steps to help you grow steadfast in faith.

Walk with Me

Step 1: Open your mind to who YOU are as a whole individual.

> The person you are when you're alone is who you truly are.

Consider the different aspects of your current stage of life, your most intricate thoughts, and your deepest feelings and answer the following questions:

Do I know who I truly am?

_____

_____

_____

_____

What does it mean to me to be a *whole* individual?

_____

_____

What does my definition of a whole individual entail?

_____

_____

Am I pleased with my discovery of who I truly am? Why or why not?

_____

_____

_____

_____

Is God pleased with who I truly am? Why or why not?

_____

_____

_____

_____

What changes come to mind in order for God and me to be pleased with my true self?

_____

_____

_____

_____

> The true you may lie deep within, looking for a way to shine through.

Above all else, guard your heart, for everything you do flows from it.

—Proverbs 4:23

Step 2: ACCEPT your life stage and reality.

> Choose to embrace rather than reject your present stage of life.

With your answers to Step 1 in mind, consider the following questions:

Do I see my life stage as a permanent burden or a temporary season?

_____

_____

_____

Do I realize that my freedom of choice to make mindful changes in my present stage is what makes this freedom a gift?

_____

_____

_____

Do I have people in my life who will hold me accountable and are in agreement with my reality?

_____

_____

Not all gifts in life are hidden, yet sometimes we doubt the gifts God has planted inside us.

What are some gifts God has planted in me that I haven't yet realized? Am I trusting that these gifts are from God?

_____

_____

_____

_____

_____

_____

Step 3: Be HONEST with yourself.

> You cannot know what you truly want until you
> know who you truly are.

With your answers to Step 2 in mind, prayerfully now, in a state of acceptance, consider the following questions. Write your answers down right now without holding back.

What one thing do I want the most?

_____

_____

Why **do I want what I want?**

_____

_____

Does the thing I want bring glory to God . . . or to myself?

_____

_____

What steps am I going to take to let God reveal to me His true intentions concerning this desire?

_____

_____

Step 4: STOP avoiding your present life stage.

> Discontentment is like poison; if you let it, it will seep into your life and ruin the natural beauty that God has in store for you in each day.

Now that you have a better idea of your deepest desires from Step 3, consider the following questions:

Am I aware of the *root* of my discontentment?

_____

_____

_____

What in my life do I genuinely believe needs to change before I will no longer feel discontented?

_____

_____

_____

Is what I desire to change a *fact* or does this desire stem from a heart of ingratitude?

_____

_____

_____

How am I going to change the extent to which discontentment influences my present?

_____

_____

_____

_____

_____

> My God will meet all your needs according to the riches of his glory in Christ Jesus.
>
> —Philippians 4:19

Step 5: Embrace the NEW you!

> Do not conform to the pattern of this world, but be transformed by the renewing of your mind. Then you will be able to test and approve what God's will is—his good, pleasing and perfect will.
>
> —Romans 12:2

With the previous four steps in mind, consider the following questions:

How do I feel after being reintroduced to myself?

_____

_____

_____

_____

_____

_____

What additional thoughts come to my mind?

_____

_____

_____

_____

Hopefully, the words to describe your current feelings include some of the following:

- *Grateful*
- *Excited*
- *Relieved*
- *Hopeful*
- *Focused*
- *Blessed*
- *Content*

After reading through this first chapter and completing this Walk with Me section, if you still do not feel any more certain about where you would begin your journey toward change or toward feeling any of the words listed above, I encourage you to go before God with your thoughts and feelings. Maybe even contact a loved one, close friend, or church member and share with them the changes you're trying to start making in your life. Ask them to pray for you, or even with you, and hold you accountable for these changes to be seen to completion. The beauty of being part of a family of believers is that you don't have to fight for inner change on your own. And if you're ready now to begin making changes but you're not yet part of a family of believers, I encourage you to get connected.

Understanding the meaning behind the concept of *identifying yourself* is essential to the effectiveness of the rest of this book. Keep in mind that making changes in your heart and life is your own responsibility. Galatians 6:1–6 offers relevant, real-life instructions:

> Brothers and sisters, if someone is caught in a sin, you who live by the Spirit should restore that person gently. But watch yourselves, or you also may be tempted. Carry each other's burdens, and in this way you will fulfill the law of Christ. If anyone thinks they are something when they are not, they deceive themselves. Each one should test their own actions. Then they can take pride in themselves alone, without comparing themselves to someone else, for each one should carry their own load. Nevertheless, the one who receives instruction in the word should share all good things with their instructor.

The key to success is not personal drive and refusal to quit—it's our committed *love for God,* our commitment to obedience to His Word, and our commitment to accountability. This transformation is what I call "going swimming" as a skilled swimmer. First comes attaining the desire and willingness to learn how to swim (embrace singlehood) and then comes the commitment to practice the skill, learning the lessons that come with the commitment.

I finally realized that once I learned how to swim according to God's guidelines, and eventually became an expert at this skill, that was the indicator to Him that I was ready to be out of the pool—leave the stage of adolescence in Christ to move deeper into maturity in Him: the ocean.

As I continued to practice the skill of embracing singlehood, the process of growth continued into further maturity—adulthood in Christ—which I believe is God's expectation of each believer. Even then, as human beings, it takes a continuum of trust and growing maturity to better understand all that God could possibly be preparing us for during the adolescence of our singlehood.

I invite you to use the terms *adolescence* and *singlehood* interchangeably—or the terms that best suit your story. It's okay to admit to your mentor (or other mature believer who is holding you accountable) that your goal is to get *out* of the pool while waiting for God to officially deem you a solid swimmer, one who has truly owned and embraced your singleness and stands ready to take on life's uncertainties, challenges, and excitements—swimming in the *ocean.* But that topic is for later time.

> Getting into a relationship with someone is *not* the reward. The reward is learning how to be truly content in Christ, regardless of our stage of life—the reward we get to keep forever.

Also keep in mind that when the desires to date, become engaged, get married, become a mother, and more are viewed in a spiritually mature, healthy, adult way, such desires and experiences can be (and likely will be) positive. But part of maturity is to remember that your earthly relationship is *not* the *ultimate* one. God should forever after be your greatest love above all others. To keep Him in the center of your earthly relationship is to maturely mirror this truth:

A cord of three strands is not quickly broken.

—Ecclesiastes 4:12

From personal experiences, I've seen how consistently rejecting my reality also negatively affected my home atmosphere, damaged close relationships, and hurt many people I love very much. Again, our personal mental health is our own responsibility, not the responsibility of any other person or group. The biggest challenges I had to overcome before seeing long-term results were not only accepting and embracing my singlehood but also *owning* it.

My prayer as you read this book is that you will realize the ultimate goal is not to end up in an earthly relationship, or even to be perfectly happy being single (for as long or short a time as that may be), but to end up in a deeper, eternal relationship with your Creator.

Does your life exemplify your faith as supported by this scripture?

> The Lord is my shepherd, I lack *nothing*!
>
> —Psalm 23:1 (author emphasis)

CHAPTER TWO

Okay, I Think I'm Ready

Learning How to Swim

It wasn't until I decided to let go and became okay with the reality of my singlehood that God started to reveal to me more of my purpose in life. In the discovery process I also found ample joy waiting for me. I had finally realized it was *time to start learning how to swim!*

Consider what the experience is like to actually go swimming. You're most likely going with friends, and the expectation is to have a good time, right? Right. Now consider what it's like to go swimming with someone who doesn't know how to swim at all. The experience immediately becomes entirely different. Instead of focusing on enjoying the outing, your attention is now solely on the person you're with, feeling responsible for the non-swimmer's safety at all times. Who would want that responsibility? Yikes!

Parallel to that imagery, imagine choosing to date someone who doesn't know the first thing about living life in singleness (swimming). Realizing this in a new relationship brings about a burden shift. Instead of you each carrying your own weight and being able to share any additional weights life *will* throw your way, you as a swimming single feel an imbalanced responsibility for the other single's emotional well-being.

Often the focus of such relationships consists of nothing more than the more mature, experienced swimmer reassuring the less experienced swimmer of their affection. In other words, the expert swimmer takes on the responsibility of the newer swimmer's emotional security in an effort to help them "feel safe at all times." This unhealthy, imbalanced parallel transpires over time as the seasoned single makes reassuring promises like "I'll never leave you" and "No matter what, I'll always care about you"—much as parents reassure their children. For individuals in this imbalanced relationship, everything can come across as loving and genuine, yet, from the outside looking in, the reality is that any relationship that reflects a parent-child dynamic emotionally will not last very long—not because they don't love each other, but because that dynamic is not the reason God puts two people together.

Side Note: Such repeated reassuring statements by the expert swimmer (seasoned single) typically stem from a conflicting place of both love and guilt in the fact that the non-swimmer adult is not yet able to trust their partner's care because they haven't yet grown up emotionally and spiritually. Most often, this particular dynamic involves the guy reassuring the girl, but every now and again it's the girl reassuring the guy. Either way, the same principles apply.

> We each need to grow as individuals into mature adults before uniting in a coupling relationship.

To avoid getting involved in imbalanced, unhealthy relationships, we must remember the reason for being in a relationship in the first place. That reason should always be to glorify God in our human uniting "as one"[1] with Christ, to "*spur one another on toward love and good deeds*,"[2] accomplishing more as a couple ("two are

1   2 Corinthians 12
2   Hebrews 10:21

34

better than one"[3]), for which God will one day reward us in heaven. (Now in contrast, not everyone wants to marry—and that's okay too! Some individuals are truly content with great close friendships and strong family bonds throughout their adult lives.)

> One cannot truly enjoy the companionship of another until both learn what it's like to be alone at the feet of Jesus.

What does this mean? I believe that when you choose someone to date, you need to be sure both of you first are able to identify who you are as individuals and to distinguish yourselves as separate identities. This task takes mastery that is honed over the course of your character development—the planting and harvesting process—throughout childhood and begins to solidify in the adolescent years and becomes solid by adulthood.

Even so, consistently positive relationships also run the risk of never detecting what may be lying beneath the surface: *codependency.* Codependency is a person's inability to be on their own or to provide care for themselves emotionally. A more concrete definition can also be considered: one who is characterized by excessive emotional reliance on another person.

Unfortunately, the discomfort of a codependent in facing the possibility of ending up alone or single again inevitably leads to a need for constant reassurance, making the relationship stressful rather than enjoyable and God-focused. In a codependent relationship, one person is attempting to teach the other person "how to swim"—in other words, trying to help the other learn how to enjoy who they are as an individual and to see all the goodness that the "swim teacher" already sees in them. The more emotionally mature partner takes this role on out of love and genuine care. However, it should be the less-experienced swimmer who first learns (prior to a relationship) to see the goodness in themselves instead

---

3   Ecclesiastes 4:9–12

of relying (in a relationship) on someone else to consistently show, reassure, and remind them. Based on my personal experiences, I believe the best thing for a couple in an imbalanced relationship to do in moving forward is to break the relationship and wait separately until the insecure and less-mature person has learned to manage life on their own. Then they may want to reconsider the idea of a relationship together. This can be done in a plethora of ways, which I'll explained in more detail later on.

> Our best teacher to provide these life lessons and assist us in our growth is God.

Discontentment in singlehood can produce self-centeredness—a serious issue in any relationship. Healthy relationships are selfless relationships formed by two people who know exactly who they are (or who they're working to become) and what they want and are okay with being on their own. In addition, the two individuals know independently what each has been called to do by God.

If we know better than to go swimming with someone who doesn't yet know how to swim, why do we get into such relationships? Why do we choose to be with someone who hasn't yet accepted their current single-life stage with contentment, who doesn't yet know who they are as an individual or have an idea what they want outside of a relationship? Unfortunately, the less experienced swimmer will ultimately end up overly dependent on the expert swimmer and will skew the quality of the relationship.

> Too often we mistaken high attraction and commitment to someone as love when in reality it's a pairing of codependent individuals who will perpetually enable unhealthy and unstable thoughts and feelings that will impair rather than empower the relationship.

Yet, this is exactly what we do. Crazy, right? You've seen this and perhaps you've done this. I have, and I've seen close friends and family enter such relationships. Anyone is fully capable of falling into this trap, but why is that? Because it's natural for us as humans to care about those around us, even those we do not know or know well. For example, if we are literally in a pool with someone who doesn't know how to swim, even if we don't know them, we would (I hope) go out of our way to keep them from drowning if we saw they were in danger, right?

But caring about someone, or being attracted to someone, or getting along with someone are not the core fundamentals to achieving healthy God-centered and God-purposed relationships. Rather, these are the bonuses.

I encourage you to take these steps to refrain from jumping into a relationship on the basis of caring, attraction, and getting along:

- Be aware of yourself and others.
- Seek advice from mentors who can see more clearly than you because they are not the ones blinded by attraction.
- Stay in prayer and God's Word for clear knowledge, wisdom, and discernment.
- Maintain accountability partners.
- Take a close look at the other person's lifestyle: behaviors and choices, interactions and reactions, interests, and closest relationships.

Why Awareness Is Critically Important

Awareness of yourself will help you

- see your own swimming pools and swimming skills;
- determine where you need to make changes in yourself and in your circumstances; and
- enable you to see whether you are making steady progress with those changes.

Awareness of potential relationship partners will open your eyes to better see

- their pool to assess (not judge) whether or not the codependent single has seen and acknowledged the need for changes in themselves and their situations;
- if the individual is actively working on those needed changes;
- if there are others in agreement with the individual's reality; and
- if there are any reoccurrences that are not beneficial. In other words, assess whether or not they have truly made lasting changes.

In my situation, I realized my actions had caused me oftentimes to be "the other person" (the codependent single) in someone else's life. It was right that those men did not choose to go swimming with me (date me). I called each guy in my life "a ledge" because even though we were in fact in a relationship (unhealthy and unofficially), I had yet to experience the feeling or satisfaction of being called someone's girlfriend. I grew to learn this was by the grace of God because I was far from ready to be someone's girlfriend. Let's face it, I was still very much a hot mess. I believe that before we can move forward in our walk with God, we must first admit to ourselves that we are a work in progress. If we trust God, we can believe He has the power to turn us into someone *beautiful, whole, and skilled enough to swim in the ocean.*

My ledge relationships were founded on what I shared earlier: feeling high attraction, thinking it was love, or hoping it would turn into love eventually when I actually was blindly and codependently pairing myself with other enablers. Naturally these relationships lasted for only a short time because I and my ledges could not sustain a *mature* or actual relationship centered in Christ. Instead, the relationships were centered in my fear of drowning (remaining single forever) when all along I should have been trusting God with my interest in men. I should have been allowing myself to embrace singlehood for the beauty and healthy growing experience it is. Notice that I did not include the word *committed* regarding those ledge relationships because there is the factor of selfishness to consider, which I came to learn personally about myself and others. Enablers can be selfish too.

Can we agree that unhealthy individuals create unhealthy relationships?

It was wrong for me and wrong for them to agree in our hearts that it was okay to have such interactions.

> It is wrong to choose to be with someone when you or they have not yet grown stable and contented in singleness or when either of you has witnessed emotional unhealthiness in the other. Such scenarios show *how enablers nurture their own gardens of discontentment.*

This is precisely why it's important to take note of our own struggles as well as the struggles of another before agreeing to be in a relationship.

> Do two walk together unless they have agreed to do so?
> —Amos 3:3

When God pairs two people, He has a far more abundant life in mind for them than simply happiness and fun times. He has a multi-layered fruitful plan that will, through the help of the Holy Spirit, enable the healthy couple to sow seeds into the lives of others to help bear good fruit in them. This was God's plan for His children all along.

> That is why a man leaves his father and mother and is united to his wife, and they become one flesh.
>
> —Genesis 2:24

God created the union of man and woman in order to accomplish His divine purposes. Healthy relationships are thereby formed by two people who have come to know the following by walking through a season of singleness with Christ as their central focus:

- Exactly who they are in Him and who He has purposed them to be
- Who they are continually working to become for His glory
- What they want in life that will further His kingdom
- That they are truly okay and unafraid being on their own with Him

If the focus of starting a relationship is not Christ-centered but self-centered, those two individuals should *not* be together. The substance of their relationship will be merely a futile attempt to temporarily satisfy themselves or an imbalanced codependent relationship in which one is caring for the other.

In contrast, healthy relationships are not self-centered and will have not only a foundational focus on Christ but also an outward focus of genuine, mutual, long-lasting care rooted in and blossoming from the care of Christ.

> Once we accept and embrace singlehood as a *healthy experience of growth and maturity,* we can free of the irrational feelings that we will be in danger or harmed by being single.

Take a moment to ask yourself these questions:

Who is "the other person" (the unhealthy person) in my life? Am I currently "the other person" to someone else?

_____

_____

Now ask yourself the harder question:

How am I going to begin today to change my circumstance?

_____

_____

I've found that when we have a better understanding of our current situation, this evaluation or reevaluation is not only spiritually beneficial but refreshing. Rather than choosing to run away from singleness and avoid it completely, we can use the tools that are effective to make our lives and relationships not only better and healthier but also more enjoyable.

At different points during my early twenties, I developed an interest in someone without considering how I was doing *spiritually*. I also often assumed the person I was developing feelings for was in a great place spiritually. Or the reverse: I would be doing fairly well spiritually but the other person waved multiple red flags that I chose to ignore. Even upon graduating from undergraduate school, I found myself often getting caught up in a pattern of doing well for long stretches in my walk with God but still keeping my eyes peeled for possible relationship interests.

This mind-set became problematic because *in my heart* I was subconsciously practicing a spiritual reward system alongside my discontentment. Have you ever experienced thoughts like mine? "Okay, God, I've been practicing purity for a few months now. I've been having my quiet times consistently; I've been leading Bible studies; I've been baptizing people . . . so where is my reward? Where is my prize, God?"

My own treat for "good Christian girl" behavior was choosing my own reward: a boyfriend! Are you laughing and nodding in agreement as you read this confession? Yes? Well, I'm glad I'm not alone.

The truth is, realizing the reality of this ugliness in our hearts is the first step toward repentance. Lord willing, with repentance and my commitment to change, there will be eventual long-lasting change.

I distinctively remember being out to lunch with a few close sisters and expressing these very thoughts and feelings. This whole entitlement and self-righteousness perspective I practiced in my heart was the undertone of just about every conversation when discussing my relationship with God. Then out of nowhere (I kid you not), a friend interrupted me mid-sentence and said, "Tatiana! You know God is not Santa Claus, right? Your prayer list sounds like a wish list!"

She was right.

How many of us treat God as if He's our Santa rather than our Savior who sacrificed His Son for our redemption? How many of us? Let's all honestly raise our hands in truth here. We genuinely think we're doing everything right and everything we need to do as disciples and expect God to grant us everything we list in our quiet time.

First John 5:14 says, "If we ask anything according to his will, he hears us." Therefore, if God hasn't answered your prayer for that brother to call you or ask you out on a date, then that wish is probably not His plan for you! But do we take the time to consider this? And do we practice surrendering to His will?

No.

What do we do instead? Often we behave exactly the way I've described my own discontentment.

Outwardly I had laughed at my friend who'd called me out on my wish list for God, and I had nodded in agreement because she had spoken truth. But my heart was still steaming with discontentment. I went back to my quiet time and continued to complain about all the things in my life I thought I lacked.

> After desire has conceived, it gives birth to sin; and sin, when it is full-grown, gives birth to death.

—James 1:15

> Walking around cute and put together on the outside but carrying a heart of stone and bitterness against God on the inside leads to spiritual death.

Do you want to continue allowing your discontentment to cause you spiritual death? We need to be actively aware of our spiritual states. *Actively* aware.

Months later I found myself going back to my quiet-time journal. I had a list of prayers I wanted answered by the end of the month! Bold and disrespectful, right? I know. Shameful. Amen. But praise God, the Lord is gracious.

One day during that self-centered season, as I was having my quiet time with the Lord, I believe the Holy Spirit said to me, "You know your prayer list is for *you* to stay on task, not for *Me* to stay on task, right?"

I tell you, my heart almost stopped and leapt out of my chest. I felt convicted. I also felt completely and entirely in awe, being called out, just like that, once again. Except this time it was coming directly from my Father. The Lord will do that. He will send people to speak directly into our lives to redirect us, and when we refuse to listen to His correction, He then comes in and delivers the same message. How often has this happened to you?

I got on my knees and said, "Okay, Holy Spirit, I understand that You're not Santa Claus, but I also know Your promise from Psalm 37:4, that if I choose to delight in You, You will give me the desires of my heart. Help me, Lord, to create and maintain a *balance*."

I threw away my monthly prayer list (checklist)—twenty-eight things I wanted for myself—and from that point forward I created a list of people I could pray for instead.

There's nothing wrong with being attracted to someone— it's normal and even healthy. But the last thing you want is to start developing and pursuing emotional interests outside God's will. If a desire to be in a relationship is so strong that it distracts you from your relationship with God and His purposes, He calls this "idolatry" and instructs us to "put to death, therefore, whatever belongs to your earthly nature: sexual immorality, impurity, lust, evil desires and greed, which is idolatry" (Colossians 3:5).

The principle of Matthew 6:24 also applies to serving ourselves over serving God:

> "No one can serve two masters. Either you will hate the one and love the other, or you will be devoted to the one and despise the other."

The apostle Paul pled with believers:

> I have often told you before and now tell you again even with tears, many live as enemies of the cross of Christ. . . . Their mind is set on earthly things.
>
> —Philippians 3:18–19

We each struggle with idolatry. My pressing desire to be in a relationship with a man was my foremost idol because that yearning exceeded my desire to be in relationship with God. We need to be honest with ourselves and God about the people and things we value more than Him, our Creator and Father. Commit to changing your focus by accepting and embracing your life stage.

Walk with Me

Step 1: ACCEPT and embrace your life stage!

God places you in various life stages for critical reasons—for you to grow, learn, and become more like Him. Please consider the following questions:

Have I accepted my current life stage? Why? Why not?

_____

_____

_____

_____

Is the acceptance of my current stage *helping me* become more like Christ? How or why not?

_____

_____

_____

_____

Do I have scriptures that support my state of acceptance? What are they?

_____

_____

_____

I encourage you to keep your list of scriptures in your wallet or use it as a bookmark in your Bible to help you keep your renewed thoughts.

When feelings of discontentment begin to creep back in, what will I do to counteract these thoughts?

_____

_____

_____

_____

Step 2: STOP choosing someone who hasn't accepted their life stage.

Sometimes our right or good ideas may not reflect God's present plans for us.

Why do I keep choosing people who haven't accepted their life stage?

_____

_____

_____

Do I seek wisdom when considering what will make me happy?

_____

_____

Sometimes we get into a relationship for the wrong reasons.

What does the Bible say about happiness versus joy?

_____

_____

Do my decisions reflect God's control over my life . . . or do they reflect my own control?

_____

_____

> Every good and perfect gift is from above, coming down from the Father of the heavenly lights, who does not change like shifting shadows.
>
> —James 1:17

When considering a potential relationship or interest, ask yourself: *Where do these ideas, opportunities, or options come from? Are they from God? Others? Myself?* Distinguishing whether they are God-led or self-initiated will give you a fresh perspective of your present and give God the opportunity to reveal to you what He really wants you to be doing and working on toward renewing your mind.

Step 3: ACCEPT your present life stage with contentment and joy.

Choosing joy instead of temporary moments of happiness is an intimate way of showing God that He is the true source of your heart's desires and a great opportunity to express your trust in Him.

> Each heart knows its own bitterness, and no one else can share its joy.
>
> —Proverbs14:10

> Nothing can change until *you* change. If change is your goal, then acceptance is the key.

Do I believe that acceptance must come first in order to move forward? Why or why not?

_____

_____

Do I have scriptures that back up my state of non-acceptance? (Hint: you shouldn't have such scriptures but instead need to repent.) What would repentance look like at this stage in my life?

_____

_____

_____

Do my actions reflect a repentant heart, ready to obey God . . . or a defiant heart that still wants to do things my own way?

_____

_____

Why am I _not_ in acceptance?

_____

_____

Step 4: Let GO of the pool ledge!

When going swimming, we naturally come up for a breath every once in a while, correct? Sometimes to see how far we've come and other times to see how much farther we have left. With this vision of swimming in mind, consider the following questions as if you're coming up for air.

> Come up for a *breath* and pay attention to the direction you're heading.

What have been the results of my obedience?

_____

_____

_____

_____

What have been the results of my disobedience?

_____

_____

_____

_____

What will it take before I'm ready to accept singleness with joy and contentment? Have these events already happened?

_____

_____

_____

_____

What have I done since those events?

_____

_____

_____

_____

(If your answer is nothing, yikes! *Just kidding!* You're still reading this book, and prayerfully the Bible, so there's still hope. Amen!)

Outside of reading, praying, and being open with my accountability partner, what initiatives have I taken to show God that I'm content and joyous about the stage I'm currently in?

_____

_____

_____

_____

Step 5: Don't turn back to the ledge; let God KEEP you afloat!

Learn how to satisfy your needs in healthy, God-honoring ways that will reap positive results.

What do I do when I can't satisfy my needs the way I want to?

_____

_____

Seeking relationships and other such attention isn't the only way we avoid the realities of being single. Some people turn to pornography, drugs, binge-watching television, overeating, excessive social media, and the like.

In what ways do I avoid my reality?

_____

_____

What healthy activities can I do instead to occupy my time?

_____

_____

_____

_____

When you start to look at negative activities that invite discontentment, *return* here instead to this list to remind yourself that you're on a path of *transformation*—new life in Christ!

Important note: Don't just occupy your time—enjoy your time! Often we can get so fixated on the changes we're making that we lose sight of the *reason* for the changes. So don't fill your schedule to the max and become overwhelmed because that will defeat the purpose. Instead, choose a few manageable additions to your healthy schedule—activities you like and will cherish in your alone time with yourself and with God.

Once the reality of your current life stage is revealed and made true for you, wait on God's timing. In the meantime, *swim!* But remember this: Just because you're in a relationship doesn't mean that the relationship is from God; it may simply be for the purpose of your further growth.

> They set up kings without my consent; they choose princes without my approval.
>
> —Hosea 8:4

Recognize the need to inquire of the Lord and wait for Him to make a presentation before you start practicing in your head the sound of your new last name!

"I warned you when you felt secure, but you said, 'I will not listen!' This has been your way from your youth; you have not obeyed me."

—Jeremiah 22:21

While swimming, be careful to make sure you're fully content in your singleness before jumping out of the water with someone, only to realize you weren't truly ready. Instead, enjoy yourself as an essential, purposed part of the bride of Christ. He's given you the tools to keep you from falling into (or back into) unhealthy pattern traps that lead to frustration and bad breakups.

> The wise prevail through great power, and those who have knowledge muster their strength. Surely you need guidance to wage war, and victory is won through many advisers.
>
> —Proverbs 24:5–6

CHAPTER THREE

Expert Swimmers in Your Life

Know Your Lifeguards

L iving a healthy lifestyle is the goal, but it's important to remember that this can't be achieved alone. Once I discovered who I truly was and what I needed to change, I was able to decide who I'd like to become. And, thankfully, God directed me to the "lifeguards" in my life—expert swimmers who help us carry out our changes.

A great way to ensure you make those changes is to be proactive to take care of yourself and enlist the healthy aid of "expert swimmers," especially in your stage of singlehood. This is the only stage in life when it's okay to be focused solely on your own emotional, mental, physical, and spiritual health. Focusing on your individual well-being will enable you to have better, healthier interactions with those around you. Collectively taking responsibility for your well-being requires your active participation in looking out for those around you too!

Unfortunately, if you don't take that proactive responsibility for yourself, the burden will be taken on by someone else, which will feed a growing dysfunction in you both and in your other relationships.

What a miserable way to continue living, never taking full responsibility for your own life.

The stage of others taking care of you is more properly known as childhood—which is very different from enlisting the help of proven lifeguards in your life. Therefore, a significant part of accepting one's singlehood is done by also owning one's *adulthood*.

> When I was a child, I talked like a child, I thought like a child, I reasoned like a child. When I became a man, I put the ways of childhood behind me.
>
> —1 Corinthians 13:11

Side Note: I'm not addressing teenagers here; my point is that a certain level of maturity must be reached for a young and maturing adult to truly own their stage of singleness. In line with my personal experiences, I've chosen to use the approach of "owning adulthood." For readers who are younger, older, and in any stage of life, feel free to apply these lessons in whatever ways best suit your circumstance and your walk with our Father.

> Being an adult has far less to do with chronological age than with emotional and spiritual maturity.

Take some time to consider if you've come to a point in life where you are owning your adulthood. Are there still some childish ways you need to change before you can honestly say to yourself, "I'm an adult"? The legitimacy of your answer will also be reflected in how others receive you and respond to you. Are you treated as and considered an adult by those close to you, including your parents or primary caregivers? Why or why not?

If you're an adult or consider yourself to be so but don't feel as though you're being treated as such, ask yourself why? What do your day-to-day behaviors convey to others? What do your day-today behaviors convey to God?

Whether you're pleased or concerned by the answers to those questions, this pivotal question is a great starting place for you: What is the disconnect between your believing you are an adult but others not treating you as such?

I urge you to test your thoughts. Go to God, and then address the individuals you feel are still treating you like a child. This exercise helped me not only to own my adulthood but also to communicate with others the growth I was striving to achieve emotionally, mentally, and spiritually.

Words cannot properly express the joyful feelings we have when God answers a specific prayer. For me personally, His revealing His power, care, and involvement in my stage of singlehood made me feel all the closer to Him. Even though we are His children, God constantly talks in His Word about our need to become *mature in Christ.* He yearns for us to become bold, courageous adult children. Think of your relationship with your parents. You will always be their child, but they don't want you to act like a child forever. God feels the same exact way about our growth toward maturity in Him.

So, if you are an adult feeling that you are being treated as an adult, that you have achieved adulthood, and that you are owning your adulthood, then congratulations! I hope these next few chapters will encourage you onward toward new levels of faith and victories in your walk with Christ.

> Not that I have already obtained all this, or have already arrived at my goal, but I press on to take hold of that for which Christ Jesus took hold of me. Brothers and sisters, I do not consider myself yet to have taken hold of it. But one thing I do: Forgetting what is behind and straining toward what is ahead, I press on toward the

goal to win the prize for which God has called me heavenward in Christ Jesus.

—Philippians 3:12–14

This same level of responsibility goes hand-in-hand with the swimming metaphor: If we as individuals are unable to care for those who can't yet swim, our typical proactive measure is to put someone else in charge of their safety—a *lifeguard*. If we share this universal protocol for an activity as simple as going swimming, why do we not take the same proactive measure in our spiritual walk? As followers of Christ, we need spiritual lifeguards in our lives, typically called disciplers, accountability partners, prayer partners, and the like.

In the beginning of my walk with God, I would seek counsel from those I expected to give me the advice my itching ears wanted to hear. Often we're tempted to do this. I would choose those I knew would be nice to me rather than truthful and teaching, those I felt comfortable confessing my sin to without feeling too intimidated. But I realized as I got older that choosing such lifeguards was not a good habit. I was not challenging myself to learn how to swim— to grow spiritually. Imagine a full-grown adult taking swimming lessons in a children's group. The techniques and exercises for children are not suitable for adult students because adults and children are in completely different stages of life. I had outgrown the type of teacher I was going to for advice, but I stayed under their care because I had grown very comfortable there. Instead of learning how to swim in that discipleship setting, I was simply nurturing my bad habit of discontentment and still holding onto the ledge.

I asked myself at this time, *How can I be more proactive in my singlehood?* The following questions will give insight into the specific steps I took.

Walk with Me

Step 1: Find expert swimmers who can help you stay FOCUSED and give you sound advice.

There are people all around you who are good at being on their own and know how to

enjoy their single life. Go find them! Be willing to learn from them. Seek advice from married couples, older singles, and family members who are proven good swimmers, and apply their advice. Be honest about how you're doing in this area of your life, not only with yourself but also with the people you're choosing to let in.

Who are the good swimmers around me? Are they in my close circle of friends?

_____

_____

_____

Step 2: Choose friends who will help you ENJOY your singlehood.

Monkey see, monkey do! If you spend all your free time with other singles who hate their stage in life, you're ultimately agreeing to continue being miserable. You know the saying, "Misery loves company."

> Do not be misled: "Bad company corrupts good *character*."
>
> —1 Corinthians 15:33 (author emphasis)

If all your closest friends are married or in relationships, the tendency to feel discontented will be greater. Make plans that involve getting your mind off yourself and on something solid and healthy that will encourage your contentment in singlehood. Discover what it means to enjoy your single stage in your own way and have fun experiencing this stage with others.

How do I plan to change my inward focus to an outward focus?

_____

_____

_____

"Whoever refreshes others will be refreshed" (Proverbs 11:25). How can I live out this scripture on a regular basis?

_____

_____

_____

Step 3: Find your BALANCE.

In your efforts to create and maintain better habits, you can take that focus to such an extreme that you end up avoiding your genuine desires. This extreme can end up hurting your ability to fully give your cares to God.

> Humble yourselves, therefore, under God's mighty hand, that he may lift you up in due time. Cast all your anxiety on him because he cares for you.
>
> —1 Peter 5:6–7

On the opposite extreme, going out and staying out every night is not the answer to enjoying singleness. There is a healthy balance between obsessing over better habits and totally abandoning those habits. Reading the life of Jesus from the New Testament gives us the supreme example of balance. One healthy and captivating activity is to spend time in the Word, discovering biblical examples to follow.

What am I learning in my personal Bible study and from those who are helping me embrace my singleness?

_____

_____

_____

Step 4: Know your HELPERS versus your hinderers.

Satan loves to distract, especially when you're trying to refocus your attention on God and His purpose for you. That is why you need to be cautious to identify your helpers versus your hinderers while continually praying for wisdom.

> Be alert and of sober mind. Your enemy the devil prowls around like a roaring lion looking for someone to devour.

—1 Peter 5:8

A hinderer is someone who simply agrees with your negative feelings about being single. This form of advice will not help you grow but rather help you nurture your discontentment. Look for true helpers, those who will speak the truth to you in love.

Also be okay with not having access to helpers at all times; it is possible to become overly dependent on your helpers.

- Reevaluate your current deepest relationships, both inside and outside the kingdom.
- List those below. (Yes, it may seem strange at first but trust me, visuals can be entirely helpful.)

Are these friendships (helpers or hinderers) drawing me closer to contentment in Christ or further away? (Note the term "helper" beside the name of each true helper.)

_____

_____

_____

_____

Step 5: KEEP on swimming!

When you're doing everything you need to be doing—listening and applying the advice you've been given—keep going! Keep practicing your lighthearted, relaxing swim, content during your wait. Be patient and be present in the wonderment of free-swimming that the Lord has invited you to ENJOY!

How have I enjoyed swimming today?

_____

_____

_____

_____

In what ways has swimming helped change my relationship with God? With others?

_____

_____

_____

_____

What is still preventing me from enjoying my swimming time?

_____

_____

_____

> "Whoever believes in me, as Scripture has said, rivers of living water will flow from within them."
>
> —John 7:38

Consider the "rivers of living water" God gifted to you. Remember that extremes are not His plan.

> In this meaningless life of mine I have seen both of these: the righteous perishing in their righteousness, and the wicked living long in their wickedness. Do not be overrighteous, neither be overwise—why destroy yourself? Do not be overwicked, and do not be a fool— why die before your time? It is good to grasp the one and not let go of the other. Whoever fears God will avoid all extremes.
>
> —Ecclesiastes 7:15–18

CHAPTER FOUR

Let Go of the Floaties!

False Support Systems

The beauty of being led by God to help others with their challenges is that He will help you get through those same areas in your own life first. Through His love and patience, He revealed to me each of my false support systems that I thought were helping me through my season of singlehood.

Like anything in life, when learning something new, we need help. This help may come in the form of a parent, friend, teacher, sibling—anyone who has already accomplished the skill. Let's consider a young child about four or five years old who has learned to swim but isn't yet ready for the deep end or to be left alone in the water. What do parents typically use that helps their children feel more independent in the pool while gaining more confidence in swimming and helps parents feel more secure about their children's safety? You guessed it! Floaties! This is much like the help we need in our process of becoming more and more independent as we move from childhood through the teen years and into adulthood, confidently and safely owning our singleness. As single adults who have grown in our skill to be confident in singleness, we must make sure we aren't still clinging to floaties.

What does this mean exactly? How do you recognize if you're clinging to a floatie? What does a floatie in singlehood look like? Well, sometimes a floatie takes the shape of things that occupy large chunks of our time, so much so that we don't notice we're not allowing ourselves the time to exercise the full capacity of our strength to live well as a single. For example, constantly working or studying can create the *illusion* of a strong-willed, independent, single person when in reality the individual just hasn't taken or been given the opportunity to discover if they're truly confident and independent as a single. Can you relate? Have you considered this before? Or do you know someone whose life looks like this?

Examples that are more common are usually negative, like being part of a close-knit clique that spends their time gossiping about everyone else, living on social media, rarely going out to interact with others, or perhaps living in laziness—an endless TV-and-snacks lifestyle. All the above, unfortunately, serve as false support systems that do not help you accomplish healthy confidence and independence as a single person. In fact, these do the exact opposite! Participating in any of these behaviors will eventually result in a lack of confidence and in dependence on things that are not beneficial to you at all.

> It's time to get rid of the time-suckers and develop habits that will help you grow into an even greater human being.

Attributes developed out of healthy habits are great contributions to your walk with Christ, and possibly one day into a relationship with that special someone.

Have you ever been in a situation where you thought you'd won a major victory, only to realize you had completely failed? It could involve passing an academic exam, achieving a spiritual goal, or anything else. Well, that was me. I came crashing down to a significant realization that radically shook my faith to my core. During the span of about two months, I had no choice but to look at myself in the mirror and decide if I was going to wholeheartedly walk my Christian walk or fall away from God.

Sometimes we can be guilty of wanting something so much that we convince ourselves, "There's no possible way God doesn't want that for me!" Unfortunately, we're at risk of doing this so often that we end up completely missing His guidance, warning signs, and hand signals against the very thing we desire. Because of our disobedience against His greater knowledge of what we truly need, He eventually has to send someone to interrupt our path and say, "Hey! This is what you *think* you're doing, but this is what is *actually* going on, and this is what I want you to do instead."

Doesn't this sound familiar? Did God not already interrupt humankind's destination? With Jesus? He sent Jesus to earth to die for your sins and mine, directing us to the path that leads us back to God.

It wasn't until I chose to repent, practice humility, and thank God for helping me decide enough is enough that He was able to start using me again. He always gives us a choice. I had come to a place where I wanted to choose to start following His lead instead of my own mental-note instructions that were leading me toward disaster.

> The lot is cast into the lap, but its every decision is from the Lord.
>
> —Proverbs 16:33

For as long as I can remember, I've had the greatest desire to pursue ministry, only to realize two things: one, my motives were not pure; and two, once they were made pure, my desire was not fit for the current season I was in. It wasn't until later that I realized I was using something positive, like the pursuit of ministry, as a *floatie* to distract me from the fact that I was not fully embracing or even accepting my singleness.

Over the years I've learned the danger in trying to force something to come about rather than seeking the covering of God and the wise counsel and blessing of others. Thankfully, God is patient and faithful, always there to redirect us when we start to veer away from Him—if we allow Him to redirect us. Learning how to allow God to move in my life—instead of obsessing over how I wanted my life to be—meant setting *my* timeline aside and choosing to enjoy *His* timeline as a journey with my Lord and Savior. In all honesty, this change in me was definitely not something that took place overnight; it took much practice and a conscious daily decision to learn how to fully rely on God rather than on the things I was comfortable with at that time in my life.

When you desire something honorable for a long while, and that thing is no longer a false support system for you, God may still not answer your prayer the way you want. But His way is always the best way.

It's important to me to be completely transparent and realistic with you because I don't want you to misunderstand the realities of my own prayer lists, nor God's Lordship over us. I do not have a long list of answered prayers of the things I've always wanted. My life consists simply of prayers that I have come to peace with. I'm doing my best to complete all the things I've come to see are truly what God has set before me for His glory, including writing this book.

> All these people were still living by faith when they died. They did not receive the things promised; they only saw them and welcomed them from a distance, admitting that they were foreigners and strangers on earth.
>
> —Hebrews 11:13

Although this verse may seem unfair, it's not. I relate very closely with this verse, especially because there are multiple desires in my life that appear to be left unreceived or unanswered by God. I've simply become content to welcome those from a distance as I continue to live by *faith*. When developing desires, we have to remember first and foremost that this world is temporary and, as many of you already know, not our permanent home. What will Jesus find you doing the day He returns to the earth or you otherwise meet Him face-to-face? Will He find you living by faith . . . or will He find you bitter about the things you think you need from Him in order to be satisfied and content but haven't received?

It simply may not be the right season for you to receive some of the things you desire. Or perhaps they are not at all what God wants for you. Whatever the case, what are your desires? Which desires are false support systems distracting you from being able to place your complete trust in God? Are you going to trust that He knows exactly what you need and the perfect time for you to receive those things? In the meantime, how are you going to trust God while you wait?

Once we've identified and grown out of our false support systems, we can use what we've learned to sustain someone else by giving them support.

> We know that in all things God works for the good of
> those who love him, who have been called according to
> his purpose.
>
> —Romans 8:28

What lessons have you learned from your experiences that you can use to help someone else?

Walk with Me

Step 1: Do it for GOD!

The first step in deciding to let go and wait for God should *not* be to receive a reward, specifically, a relationship. The benefit of letting go is being able to be on your own and content on your own.

How is God the center of the changes in my life?

_____

_____

Does my willingness to change reflect that I truly believe God is enough to sustain me?

_____

_____

Am I turning to God when tempted to cling to my ledges again or wanting my floaties back?

_____

_____

Step 2: Decide today what your CONSISTENCY will look like.

To keep your focus on Christ, you must continue to look to Christ! I encourage you to do the following:

- Don't quit!
- Don't say it's too hard.
- Develop a game plan that will prevent you from becoming distracted.
- Place sticky notes of various Bible verses on your mirror or desk—even on the back of your phone—to help remind you what your focus *should* be!

How well did I stay focused today?

_____

In what ways am I allowing myself to be distracted? What distractions do I need to get rid of?

_____

_____

_____

How have I maintained consistency in staying focused?

_____

_____

What are some ways I can grow in consistency?

_____

_____

_____

Step 3: Identify your weaknesses and turn them into STRENGTHS.

As a follower of Christ, your goal is to look more like Him—by emulating His character.

What things, people, and circumstances in my life are preventing me from trusting God?

_____

_____

When am I going to decide to cut those off and let go of them?

_____

_____

When I become free of distractions, who am I going to share this spiritual victory with?

_____

_____

_____

Step 4: Swim as if no one is WATCHING!

Remember that God's opinion of you is the only opinion that matters. When you find yourself becoming stressed about the opinions of others and thereby working on changes to please *them*, rather than *God*, that's a sign you're changing for the wrong reason.

Don't put a time limit on how long you're going to enjoy your singleness. That is God's decision, not yours.

How am I going to trust God's timing?

_____

_____

Even when you find yourself doing well for a while, don't get distracted by what's going on around you.

How am I going to continue being free from distractions?

_____

_____

_____

If you don't receive praise for your growth, don't be upset. Remember that God, not humankind, is the one who is preparing you in every season.

How can I know that I'm doing this for Him and not for the praises of others?

_____

_____

_____

_____

Step 5: Remember that even though change starts with you, it's NOT all about you!

Your victories in changing should benefit more than just yourself. Your obedience to Christ should have a domino effect that prompts change in others.

Have my changes made positive impacts in the lives of those around me? How?

_____

_____

_____

Who can I help, and who have I helped, to have spiritual victories as I've been working on myself?

_____

_____

Where is God starting to lead me next on my journey of change?

_____

_____

Am I still listening to His voice? How can I be sure of this? (Hint: by obeying the Scriptures)

_____

_____

CHAPTER FIVE

You Have Lungs— Use Them!

Being Okay with Asking or Screaming for Help

Sometimes God gives you a vision that no one else can see. That's when you have to decide to trust in Him and just go with it. In the midst of making my own positive changes, I found that I still felt really alone and as though I had no support. Through much prayer, God showed me that if I kept asking for help, He'd send help to me.

> "Ask and it will be given to you; seek and you will find;
> knock and the door will be opened to you."
>
> —Matthew 7:7

Sometimes we allow pride to get in the way of asking when we know we need the help of others. Unfortunately, pride can lead us to making worse mistakes than if we had opened up to a mentor about our failures in the beginning.

If you go to the same mentor, a spiritual lifeguard for example, with the same issue over and over again and still nothing is changing, it's normal to feel discouraged. And you may feel pressure to grow spiritually at a faster rate because you don't want to let your lifeguard down or feel as though you're wasting their time. That was me for a really long time. This negative thinking is just one of Satan's schemes to prevent our growth process. Thankfully, the Lord freed me from the temptation to people-please and instead embrace the freedom of being authentic in my faith with those who care most about me and my spiritual journey. He can do the same for you.

It's okay to go to your lifeguard (accountability partner) for the same thing repeatedly until a heart change happens in you. In the unfortunate event that your mentor tells you that you can no longer come to them about persistent issues, I encourage you to gently ask why. Be prepared to receive their answer with grace and with trust in God that He will be faithful to provide you with another lifeguard.

Isn't it surreal that even when our minds are willing to obey God, our flesh may still not be ready? Even the apostle Paul, who dedicated his life to bringing people to Jesus, shared in Romans 7:19–25 his struggle with this very issue. Yet he made evident changes that were clear to others. A new life in Christ will be evident to others. I encourage you to read that passage. The apostle Paul also said, "If anyone is in Christ, the new creation has come: The old has gone, the new is here" (2 Corinthians 5:17).

This scenario is much like understanding the concept of a new task but not training our bodies or minds to perform the task. Practical examples are learning how to ride a bike, tie our shoes, score in a sport game, drive—or swim. I certainly didn't enjoy the task of learning how to swim (grow) in my season of singleness. My lack of knowledge made me feel inadequate and like a fake. Making changes and learning something new can be very difficult.

There is a significant difference between practicing openness with an accountability partner and allowing ourselves to simply grow comfortable in sin. In 2 Corinthians 7, the apostle Paul spoke of this as well—the blatant difference between worldly and godly sorrow. For example, if you continue to go to your accountability partner week after week while continuing in sin, there is a heart issue, an unwillingness to repent and "put off your old self" (Ephesians 4:22). If you're actively in the Word, fasting, praying, being open about your sin, and purposefully working to think and behave like Christ, change will become evident in you through the Holy Spirit and in your outward behaviors.

Even then, every once in a while you will fall or stumble. You will, because you're human. But still you have a choice whether or not to continue in sin. Paul addresses this in Romans 6. Here is a personal example: Even while writing this book, and as I continued to grow in my walk with God, I began to learn and understand exactly what He wanted me to do. I chose to take those steps even if they took my out of my comfort zone—just as I had to practice riding my bike and tying my shoes. Admittedly, there were times when I still felt uncomfortable and wanted to turn back to what I was used to because it was easier. I understood why I was going through the circumstances I was in. I chose to be open and honest with those around me and developed new convictions regarding my skewed way of thinking and my need to rely on the Holy Spirit and God's Word as my ultimate sources of direction and sustainment.

Even so, I continued to struggle with accepting my singleness. I would sit at church on Sundays, be moved by a sermon, have a quiet time the next morning, go in to work, feel as if I'd given my all, come home, pray to God for hours or spend time with friends or family, and be genuinely grateful for their company. However, when it came time for me to be alone, I still wanted to return to what was familiar: my ledges and floaties. I had to consciously resist the temptation to turn to men in my fellowship group at church, resist the desire to flirt with guys I saw while out running errands, and even resist "checking in" with longtime guy friends from time to time "just to say hi." I found myself not only struggling but also *spiraling,* even though I knew my discontentment wouldn't allow me reach the goal of owning my singleness and being content in that season. That's why I wrote this book, to share with you this secret: Only by God's grace was I able to have victories during those trials and temptations. *I chose to ask for help* as many times as I needed to achieve a real change of heart and way of thinking. It's as simple as that! *Purposed persistence to renew my mind to think like Christ.*

A secret to success as a single person—and anything we set out to conquer—is having genuine believers help us along the way and hold us accountable. But here's the catch: You have to *ask* for the help you need! Once you finally ask for that help, you have to keep asking. *Keep asking!* And once you've gotten the hang of asking, continue to work on asking.

Even though I had women who knew exactly where I was spiritually, once I started making

changes, I realized that others knowing my spiritual condition wasn't enough to keep me moving forward on God's path for me. I had to constantly train myself to continue to be open and transparent about my struggles and to be okay with feeling embarrassed for a little while, because I realized my salvation *depended* on my continual repentance! As I continued to receive help, I quickly learned that I'd rather face embarrassment for a few moments than spend eternity permanently separated from God because I had chosen to live a prideful life. If my desire was truly to bring glory to God and ultimately be with Him someday in heaven, what did I have to lose by opening up to and learning from the lifeguards He'd placed in my life?

What are some things I need to scream out for help for? Or am I just allowing Satan to keep attacking me every chance he gets when I'm alone?

_____

_____

_____

_____

Walk with Me

Step 1: Be MINDFUL about your helpers.

Even in the kingdom of God, not everyone wants to see you do well. This unfortunate reality is because Satan can still creep in and use the jealousy of others to destroy your growth.

Where is my heart concerning gaining assistance?

_____

_____

Who am I going to for help? Does this person really want to see me do well or do they make me feel more anxious after opening up? (Honestly, this is a real thing we all should consider when receiving help with anything.)

_____

_____

_____

_____

Have I allowed God to reveal the lifeguards He has purposed to be my helpers?

_____

Am I allowing myself to be completely transparent with them or am I allowing my pride to get in the way?

_____

_____

How can I ask God to reveal my heart in the specific area of pridefulness?

_____

_____

Step 2: TRUST God's helpers in your life and don't be paranoid.

Satan can easily warp the need to be cautious and turn a potential lifeguard relationship into something destructive. Don't let this happen to you!

Am I praying for wisdom before going to others for help? Has their advice had positive or negative results? Why?

_____

_____

_____

_____

_____

_____

Am I sharing the whole truth with my lifeguard so I can get the best advice?

_____

What can possibly be getting in the way of my sharing the whole truth with my accountability partner? Am I first being honest with myself regarding the things I'm sharing, so I can then be honest with my helper?

_____

_____

_____

_____

Step 3: Consider WHY you are asking for help in the first place.

Don't seek help simply to gain insight that might help toward fulfilling your hope of entering a romance with the person you have your eye on. Remember that the focus of help is to keep your eyes fixed on Jesus and to allow Him to take care of the rest.

Pay attention to Satan's deceitfulness and assess if your heart is pure and receptive to the help God is providing through His people.

Is my heart pure and receptive to God? Why or why not?

_____

_____

What am I still holding onto out of fear that God won't come through?

_____

_____

Do I trust that God knows my desires better than I do? Why or why not?

_____

_____

How have I gone about showing God how much I trust Him and appreciate His guidance?

_____

_____

_____

_____

Step 4: It's okay to CRUSH on those around you; just don't let it crush you.

Feelings and physical sensations like butterflies are natural responses; however, it's what we do with these that shows whether we're allowing God to be in control. When you find yourself with feelings for someone while staying focused on God, be honest about this with your lifeguard. Don't hide your feelings and experiences from those seasoned swimmers God has placed in your life. Remember that sometimes feelings are simply something for you to learn from and not necessarily an indicator you should jump-start a romantic relationship. Consider the following:

Am I continuing to practice complete honestly in all areas of my life, including my feelings? If not, why do I feel the need to suppress the truth?

_____

_____

_____

_____

Let God, through the lifeguards He has sent your way, help you navigate through your emotions while glorifying Him with your daily actions.

Am I at peace with the fact that my feelings may not be for the purpose of getting into a relationship at this time?

_____

_____

What would being at peace with this reality look like in my daily life?

_____

_____

Side Note: Sometimes God uses even official relationships (supported by wise counsel) for learning experiences and not necessarily to prepare a couple for marriage to each other. We will get further into this topic later in the book.

Step 5: Share your TRIGGERS with your helpers.

Don't allow anything to resurface that will cause you to return to your old way of thinking.

> We know that our old self was crucified with him so that
> the body ruled by sin might be done away with, that we
> should no longer be slaves to sin—because anyone who
> has died has been set free from sin.
>
> —Romans 6:6–7

I encourage you to reread this verse before moving to the following questions. Understanding this passage is a critical aspect of what will help you continue moving forward and not revert to old habits. If there is something you don't understand about these verses, talk with your discipling partner or another believer who provides counsel for you. Remember that Christ died so we may live a new life as believers.

Now that I have a clearer perspective of the reason behind my current stage of life, what am I going to do with it?

_____

_____

_____

_____

With the perspective of Christ dying for me, what's keeping me from enjoying my current life stage?

_____

_____

_____

Tell your helpers what your triggers are—things that make you want to run back to the unhealthy habits that made you feel good when trying to avoid the reality of singleness.

What are my triggers?

_____

_____

_____

Am I honestly doing and feeling better, or am I putting on a show to get what I want in the end? (Remember, whether or not you're honest with yourself, God will make the truth clear over time.)

_____

_____

What you should want the most after reading this book is to spend eternity with God, with or without a relationship being part of your life. So, before starting a relationship, ask yourself these questions:

Have I completely surrendered my heart and feelings over to God?

_____

_____

Am I okay if God's plan is that I remain single?

_____

_____

_____

How can I glorify God with what He's already blessed me with in this present season He's allowing me?

_____

_____

_____

Even when you experience feelings for someone, and those butterflies, you can use this season to bring glory to God.

> There is a time for everything, and a season for every activity under the heavens.
>
> —Ecclesiastes 3:1

CHAPTER SIX

So You Think You Can Swim?

When Tests and Trials Hit

One of the greatest ways to show your love to God is simply to trust Him and all He is doing. Clinging to Him for dear life rather than yet another ledge is the only way to stay afloat.

Learning how to hear and honor the Lord's voice above our own, or above what our flesh wants, is not something we naturally do or easily master. It's a decision we must choose to remake each day for the rest of our lives. One morning I woke up thinking, *God, what do You have me doing? How am I going to do this? When are You going to confirm that this is definitely what You want?*

That's when I chose to allow faith to take its part in His plan. I've learned that our faith in God fills the spaces along our paths when it's difficult to trust Him because we're unsure how our experiences will all connect. We may hesitate during uneasy times and not want to continue forward, but remaining focused on God's goals for us will help us reach those goals.

When circumstances seem unclear or impossible, the temptation to do things our own way may seem more desirable. It's much easier to move forward when we can see what's in front of us. Makes sense, right? However, I've learned that when I come to uncertain places in my walk with God, I must actively remind myself that doing life my own way is an act of defiance and disobedience. Just as there were consequences as children when we disobeyed our parents, God disciplines us because He loves us so much.

> Endure hardship as discipline; God is treating you as his children. For what children are not disciplined by their father?
>
> —Hebrews 12:7

In my own times of disobedience to God, when I was not ready to listen to Him and pushed the limits, I faced the consequences of my sin: loneliness, separation from God, loss of friendships (even in the body of Christ) and family relationships, feeling rejected and depressed. My heart got so ugly I was blinded to the fact that my heart no longer looked like God's heart, all because I was unwilling to let Him be my heavenly Father. I would open my mouth and say, "Jesus is Lord," but my actions would constantly reveal that Tatiana was lord of her life. I was not yet practicing deep, raw, and honest surrender.

Surrender is arguably one of the hardest things for a human being to accomplish—not because we fear failing but because we fear being let down by someone we're counting on. But what is it about the fear of being let down that makes it such a challenge to face? Because when we're let down, trust is usually lost soon after. I'm here to share with you that Satan is the one who wants you to feel let down by God, but God has not let you down and never will. Keep counting on Him.

Jesus looked at them and said, "With man this is impossible, but with God all things are possible."

—Matthew 19:26

I would much rather be disciplined by God out of His love for me than the alternative: being mistreated by the world and feeling useless from having more love for myself and what I want than love for God and wants He wants for me—His very best.

> In your struggle against sin, you have not yet resisted to the point of shedding your blood. And have you completely forgotten this word of encouragement that addresses you as a father addresses his son? It says, "My son, do not make light of the Lord's discipline, and do not lose heart when he rebukes you, because the Lord disciplines the one he loves, and he chastens everyone He accepts as His son."

—Hebrews 12: 4–6

> No discipline seems pleasant at the time, but painful. Later on, however, it produces a harvest of righteousness and peace for those who have been trained by it.

—Hebrews 12:11

I had to train my mind to consider these verses quite often while learning to accept and own my singleness. I also had to accept God's training. I had to actively remember that whenever I was going through a test or trial, that was God's way of reminding me that I still belonged to Him, He still loved me, He wanted what's best for me, and He wanted me to trust in His plan.

Much like walking down a path, we may see the large circular stones and have an idea of where the trail is leading. But when the stones seem farther apart and we question how we'll make it across, we need faith to connect the steps and make it possible for us to continue forward.

I made my initial attempts as a hopeful and eager young woman toward owning my adulthood by seeking after my own independence emotionally, mentally, and financially. I kept in mind that I still needed deep relationships within God's kingdom as I strived to obtain a lifestyle that reflected my newfound way of thinking. While doing so, I realized I had feelings for someone. Based on my new maturity, I wanted to believe I could handle more than just feelings—I could take on the responsibility of having an actual dating relationship. But one thing I was able to learn in my teenage years as a young disciple is that even though I had passed some trials in life, that didn't necessarily mean I was ready to move on to the next life lesson. I had to learn to let God take me there, and I chose to hand my newly discovered feelings over to Him because I didn't want those feelings to be a distraction nor risk them becoming yet another temporary ledge. I wanted God to trust me too and to allow His work in me to move and develop those feelings into something more, something sustainable that would last and be used to glorify Him.

The process of transitioning to a new mind-set is not the easiest. I entered a season where I had to learn how to start becoming mentally, emotionally, and financially independent. For me, that meant *no more* coming home at the end of a long day and bawling my eyes out to whoever would listen. Those times typically included my feeling self-focused and discontented and complaining about my single life. Transitioning meant coming home and striving to be a light to those around me, learning how to give to those I lived with, appreciating their company, and choosing to rely on God to sustain me. It meant handing all my worries to Him. I had to learn how to channel my emotions so I would no longer allow them to get the best of me when I felt tempted to give in.

With much practice, I found that my mind-set was changing a lot, my focus was becoming more mature, and I was leaning on God and inquiring of Him before making even the smallest decisions.

Whether you turn to the right or to the left, your ears will hear a voice behind you, saying, "This is the way; walk in it."

—Isaiah 30:21

So, once you step out in faith, how do you continue *walking* by faith?

Walk with Me

Step 1: LOOK before you leap!

Before stepping out, be certain that step is the one God wants you to take. Go back to Scripture and also pray about the decisions you feel He is leading you to make. Spend much time asking God to make the answer abundantly clear to you and for Him to do what only He can do.

Do my decisions honor God and bring Him glory, or do they bring me—or even someone else—glory?

_____

_____

_____

Side Note: Being certain of God's direction encompasses everything, not just dealing with emotions, and is crucial throughout your entire life, not just in singlehood. You should always feel you can go to God for advice and include Him in even the smallest decisions. He wants to be a part of your decisions! You just have to let Him.

Step 2: TRUST His answer.

Because you're human, sometimes you're wrong in what you think the answer is. If you start to question or second-guess yourself, consider that God's way of redirecting you.

Is this God telling me I should wait?

_____

Forcing a situation out of His timing always ends in heartache, disappointment, and even more discontentment.

Am I trusting His timing . . . or am I pushing my own agenda here?

_____

Learn to be okay with being uncomfortable. God's control of a situation doesn't mean you're going to feel good about it 100 percent of the time. He opens and closes doors for a reason.

Am I being still and letting God work? Or am I being impatient? Possibly ungrateful?

_____

_____

_____

When God closes a door to an opportunity you thought was open to you, then trust that it wasn't the door for you to enter.

How do I respond when things like this happen?

_____

_____

If I am disappointed, was I really practicing true contentment in the first place?

_____

_____

Step 3: Don't forget to FOLLOW up.

Once we get the hang of something, we tend to feel as if we don't need help anymore. Don't be that person.

Once you start to notice victories and sense that feelings of loneliness are fading, don't hesitate to share these realizations with those around you! Be sure to go back to your lifeguards and say, "Hey, this is where I am right now; this is how I'm feeling about this situation. What do you think?" Asking questions along these lines to someone who has been helping you help yourself—and especially asking God—will keep you on the path He wants you to take.

What questions should I ask my lifeguard today?

_____

_____

_____

Am I being just as consistent in meeting together and asking for help now as I was in the beginning?

_____

_____

Am I following up with God and sharing my feelings and victories with Him too? If not, why?

_____

_____

_____

Am I still longing for God just as much now as I was before starting this process?

_____

_____

_____

Side Note: Keeping in step with the Holy Spirit is just as important as staying on the same page

as your lifeguards. God placed them in your life for a reason, so if you begin to feel as though you're ready to start swimming in the deep end or to move on to the next thing, be sure to *ask* first. Remember, there's nothing wrong with asking questions. Asking doesn't make you any less of an adult or a person with any less ownership of your singlehood. If anything, asking shows a sign of maturity, that you are growing in your overall character.

Step 4: Inquire MORE.

When God starts to reveal something to you, that's the time to run to Him all the more for further instruction. Pray for your heart to desire what God desires.

If I know what truly pleases the Lord, am I doing these things?

_____

_____

Am I storing up spiritual victories for myself or sharing with others the impact that living for God is having on my life?

_____

_____

_____

"For my thoughts are not your thoughts, neither are your ways my ways," declares the Lord. "As the heavens are higher than the earth, so are my ways higher than your ways and my thoughts than your thoughts. As the rain and the snow come down from heaven, and do not return to it without watering the earth and making it bud and flourish, so that it yields seed for the sower and bread for the eater, so is my word that goes out from my mouth: It will not return to me empty, but will accomplish what I desire and achieve the purpose for which I sent it."

—Isaiah 55:8–11

Step 5: Don't ask, just DO.

When you start to build your trust in God, He starts to build more trust in you. He will instruct you and trust you with more responsibilities as your faith in Him grows.

Have I counted the cost of living for God while enjoying my singleness? What does this look like for me personally?

_____

_____

_____

_____

_____

Even when I don't fully understand, am I going to follow Him and swim by faith?

_____

_____

_____

_____

If we are faithless, he remains faithful, for he cannot disown himself.

—2 Timothy 2:13

We must remember our "soul" and "sole" purpose is to live for Christ and share with others about Jesus. What better way to do this and remember this purpose than to live it out? In everything you do, represent Christ. In every stage of your life, remain focused on Him. When you remember why you're here, you'll forget that you're single and remember that you're a part of the bride of Christ.

God will show you all you need to accomplish during your singlehood. Consider this: If you allow the desire for a human relationship to distract you from fulfilling God's purpose for you, then why would God place you in a relationship, only to be *more* distracted? When this realization was made clearer to me, I found I was understanding God so much more in an intimate way, and I grew to not only trust His timing but also appreciate it.

> Yet he saved them for his name's sake, to make his power known.
>
> —Psalm 106:8

God wants us to be victorious in *everything* we do while living on this earth, and that can be done only through our reliance on the Holy Spirit. We must remember that these victories may not be what the world considers victories—such as wealth, fame, and glamour. Nonetheless, constantly choose to put your hope in God, no matter what, regardless of the situation. Doing this reaps eternal victories. He has chosen you to make His power known in this lost world. Never let anyone cause you to forget that.

CHAPTER SEVEN

Lifeguard in Training

Helping Others While Growing

Noticing bad habits is one thing but breaking them is another. Getting the hang of breaking my bad habits was a huge accomplishment, but I didn't want to stop there. I started helping those around me I thought could use some assistance with their "swimming" technique.

Often it's easier to find the weaknesses in someone else than in ourselves. What I found most helpful was praying that God would reveal to me the weaknesses in *my* character so I could work on those. Here is what I've learned (I'm sure you've heard this before): be careful what you pray for!

After many months, my heart, character, and mind-set were completely transformed and continued to be as I allowed expert swimmers into my life and continued to place my faith in God. I had sisters all around me sharing how much they'd seen me grow as I experienced different hardships yet still clung to God for my comfort and guidance. Although I had started working toward mental, emotional, and financial independence, as time passed, I became really sick. Another trial.

Going back and forth to the doctor trying to figure out what was wrong while working two jobs only added to my already stressful state. Soon after, I realized I had (admittedly) made a mistake in a financial area of my life where I thought I was "stepping out in faith." In truth, I had been irresponsible and should have asked for advice before trying to figure it out on my own. Yet another trial, except this one was self-inflicted. So, in the midst of illness, doctor visits, and pulling extra hours at work, each night I had to find a different way to cope with what I was going through until everything was resolved. When I tell you I had every opportunity to lash out, be angry, emotionally run back to my go-to ledges, or pout and do nothing—boy, there were definitely moments when I sure wanted to and I was so tempted! Instead, I decided to be thankful during these trials and continue pursuing the Lord and what I knew He wanted me to be doing.

> Consider it pure joy, my brothers and sisters, whenever you face trials of many kinds, because you know that the testing of your faith produces perseverance.
>
> —James 1:2–3

Side Note: I understand that I am being entirely vague about this particular area of my life. As an author, my desire is nothing less than be completely vulnerable with all of you; however, the details of my experience would shift the focus of this book. I hope to share with you in the future more in-depth details of my personal story and the ways the Lord completely changed my life. What I can say, though, is that my illness was not severe. I had unfortunately reacted to something in my environment and I am thankful to the doctors who were able to assist me. After about six weeks I returned to good health, and the Lord's faithfulness continued.

Even though I felt as though I had finally accomplished my biggest victories—becoming mentally, emotionally, and financially independent and owning my adulthood—it was not easy then to be in such a humbling circumstance, having to rely so much on others for help. In hindsight, I see how God used the experience to remind me that even though I can grow as an adult, I will always be His child. He is my ultimate provider and the perfect parent. He establishes my steps and keeps me on the right path.

> Do not be wise in your own eyes; fear the Lord and shun evil. This will bring health to your body and nourishment to your bones. Honor the Lord with your wealth, with the firstfruits of all your crops; then your barns will be filled to overflowing, and your vats will brim over with new wine. My son, do not despise the Lord's discipline, and do not resent his rebuke, because the Lord disciplines those he loves, as a father the son he delights in.
>
> —Proverbs 3:7–12

During this trying season, while spending ample time with my sisters (women in my campus ministry), I had even more opportunities to see how much God was meeting my every need. God showed this to me through frequent invitations to join in on sleepovers, extended quiet times on the beach, long prayers over the phone, and honestly just getting a chance to see more closely how each sister was living out her faith in God on a daily basis. God used this time of my need to rely more on the body of Christ and to build *deeper* relationships within it.

> God has put the body together, giving greater honor to the parts that lacked it, so that there should be no division in the body, but that its parts should have equal concern for each other. If one part suffers, every part suffers with it; if one part is honored, every part rejoices with it.
>
> —1 Corinthians 12:24–26

I learned even more so during this time that when we go to church with someone on Sundays and for midweek services or hang out after Friday devotionals, we are seeing only a single side of that person. It's a completely different experience to witness a person's life from within their home, with family, in the middle of their work routine, or when they are going to a class, work, and other events. Some find it a challenge to make time for the Lord each day, especially when their regular routine is interrupted. I had to really pray to be grateful and allow God to help me overcome my internalized emotions that made me feel as if I were an inconvenience to others in this time of need. Instead of being upset or cranky, I decided to use that time in my life to be thankful to the Lord and continue spending quality time with sisters I hadn't seen much a while. I wanted to spend extra hours in my Bible. I also wanted to come up with interesting ways to share my faith, so I started reaching out to different women at work.

During this time God revealed even more to me: what was going on in different sisters' lives, our ministry as a whole, and the need for more unity in the kingdom of God amongst the younger generation, who tend be a little too spread out at times. He showed me all the ways I could be serving Him and others instead of serving myself on social media, by sleeping **excessively**, or in daydreaming about dating someday. He helped me see that there are so many more important things going on in life than what Tatiana wanted or thought she needed. More importantly, God helped me realize how little I truly needed on a practical level to get through daily life and have really successful and encouraging days. In the midst of my character and heart transformation, my priorities and what I thought was most important were being transformed as well.

Another interesting thing I discovered during this time was that God's timing is so perfect. He

knows exactly what we need and when we need it, including the lessons we need to learn. In the midst of feeling entirely uncomfortable that my life was up in the air, I was hearing a lot of sermons on money and the way we as Christians should view it. I learned to be grateful for these biblical perspectives because everything I had been taught about money both directly and indirectly was not necessarily biblically sound.

Moreover, I was in such a vulnerable state that my focus was, thankfully, redirected in a huge way. But God will only redirect us if we *allow* Him to. He doesn't force us to do anything but honors the free will He gifted to us. Being uncomfortable for a season helped me be more open with sisters and share what was going on in my life because I really needed their help. It made me realize too that we can have a false sense of independence when we subconsciously rely on unhealthy things to meet our emotional needs. We might formulate a false sense of security because we have a job or because we are in school and go to church regularly. We can come to think that we have life all figured out and thereby eventually stop going to one another for help. This unhealthy mind-set unfortunately prevents us from going through trials *together* and learning and growing together, which is what God intended for His church all along.

> God has placed the parts in the body, every one of them, just as he wanted them to be. If they were all one part, where would the body be? As it is, there are many parts, but one body. The eye cannot say to the hand, "I don't need you!" And the head cannot say to the feet, "I don't need you!" On the contrary, those parts of the body that seem to be weaker are indispensable, and the parts that we think are less honorable we treat with special honor.
>
> —1 Corinthians 12:18–23

With this passage in mind, how can you change from being too self-focused to realizing the survival skills you need and possess are within the very body of Christ? How can you learn to become both independent in Christ and be used by God to benefit those around you, His kingdom?

Walk with Me

Step 1: Identify your SKILLS.

Get a clear idea of what you're doing, both intentionally and unintentionally, and learn how to do even better, even with those things you're already doing well.

Often we have talents we don't perceive as talents, and, unfortunately, we end up not using them. Don't let your gifts go to waste! The things that just "come naturally" to you are not a coincidence! God has a purpose for everything He planted inside you!

> Every good and perfect gift is from above, coming down from the Father.
>
> —James 1:17

| Use *all* your gifts to advance God's kingdom! |

In what additional ways can I go to God and others to further understand the difference between spiritual gifts, natural talents, and strengths?

_____

_____

_____

_____

Use the journal area for these steps:

1. List things you are good at (natural talents and strengths) and what you've come to discover are your spiritual gifts.
2. Beside each, note how you have been using each attribute.
3. Note if you are using that attribute only for yourself, and if so, why.

My Attributes   How I Am Using Them

_____ _____

_____ _____

_____ _____

_____ _____

_____ _____

_____ _____

_____ _____

_____ _____

_____ _____

_____ _____

_____ _____

Which of these am I using only for myself and why?

_____

_____

_____

How can I use this list to advance God's kingdom instead of just for myself?

_____

_____

_____

_____

Side Note: Galatians 6:7–8 says, "Do not be deceived: God cannot be mocked. A man reaps what he sows. Whoever sows to please their flesh, from the flesh will reap destruction; whoever sows to please the Spirit, from the Spirit will reap eternal life." As you embark on the next steps of your journey with Christ, I urge you to keep in mind that even when it comes to using your gifts, you reap what you sow. Be mindful that you can also reap negative results—not the positive results you originally intended. It's okay to be excited about identifying your gifts and talents, but if you go about using your gifts with the wrong heart, that will lead to an unwanted harvest of things you did not desire to grow in your life. This can be dangerous.

Sometimes the desire to serve can be so strong that we forget to first seek God and be led by Him. Instead, we first ask others what ways we can help in a ministry. Although asking others is great and honorable, the danger in being overly zealous is that we run ahead of God without His clear and concise direction. Moving ahead of God is moving without His navigation. I have made this very mistake, which is why I urge you to be *mindful* to first and foremost seek God and be led by Him.

Self-awareness is a key component to being effective in God's kingdom. Identifying your strengths and understanding your expectations and the expectations of others will develop not only unity but also harmony among those you are serving with and receiving guidance from.

Step 2: Create a BALANCE.

When gifted with a lot of strengths, you can easily become either too focused on yourself and self-improvement or too focused on others and trying to fix them. Pray to have a balance between the two extremes. Allow enough time to work on your personal character and weaknesses while still being able to notice the needs of others and help meet those needs where and when God leads you.

What are some ministry needs I have noticed?

_____

_____

How can I help meet these needs?

_____

_____

_____

_____

_____

Ask God to direct you to which need(s) He wants you to help meet. Remember that He wants you to maintain a balance of time in your life and will not ask you to overextend yourself. Allow Him to reveal the ways He wants you to serve, how often, and for how long and note those here.

Where God wants	How often	For how long

Once you've developed a good balance and have a clearer understanding of what you're good at and what area of service God is directing you to, then you might go to a ministry leader and share, "Hey, these are my strengths; this is how I'd like to serve."

What are some ways I can help? To whom do I need to share my interest in serving? (List those individuals.)

_____

_____

_____

Step 3: Stay humble, stay humble, stay HUMBLE.

> Do not think of yourself more highly than you ought.
>
> —Romans 12:3

Always check your heart. Even when God starts to reveal all the ways you can serve His kingdom, it's important to continuously be pure in heart.

> The heart is deceitful above all things and beyond cure. Who can understand it? "I the Lord search the heart and examine the mind, to reward each person according to their conduct, according to what their deeds deserve."
>
> —Jeremiah 17:9–10

> Don't get carried away when God has already saved the day!

Don't get carried away in pride by coming up with your own answers and solutions when God has already given you answers in His Word to every question you could ever ask. It is a privilege to be a part of and serve in God's kingdom.

With regard to humility, remember that we're all called to serve, so we're not unique in that way, but you might simply discover one of yours gifts a little sooner than someone else finds theirs.

How am I going to make sure I stay humble as God reveals my gifts and talents to me?

_____

_____

_____

As I begin to walk in my purpose, serving God's kingdom, how will I refrain from becoming prideful?

_____

_____

_____

How will I keep myself in check spiritually?

_____

_____

_____

Remember that with new strengths come new weaknesses. Don't allow the devil to keep you blindsided from this inevitable reality. As you reach each different life stage, it will come with its own set of challenges and victories, new to what you've known before.

> The purposes of a person's heart are deep waters, but one who has insight draws them out.
>
> —Proverbs 20:5

Side Note: Be aware of Satan's attacks! Remember that the devil prowls around like a roaring lion who doesn't want to see awesome, healthy, zealous disciples ready and eager to serve, so he's going to plant fear in us and try to make us doubt our *God-given* strengths and talents to prevent us from reaching our greatest potential in life! This is why you must be intentional and consistent in prayer and ask God where your particular gifts can be used.

Step 4: Learn how to TEACH.

In order to teach, you must first learn how to be taught. The best learning experiences are often mutual. When you find yourself sharing or teaching something you've mastered, be prepared to learn from the individuals you are teaching as well. As we've often heard in one form or another, one must first learn to follow the rules before instructing others to abide by them. When teaching those around you, always keep your heart and mind like that of a growing student—one who is humble and eager to learn.

What are some ways I have been able to teach others recently?

_____

_____

_____

What is something I can learn from those I am currently teaching?

_____

_____

_____

How can I help the person I'm teaching learn to teach others?

_____

_____

_____

Something to consider just for fun: as we learn to rely more on Christ and one another, we all become *stronger* as believers.

Why do I think God constructed His church to be connected to Him and others in this way?

_____

_____

_____

What the world may see as a weakness, God sees as the opposite. Share this thought with a friend!

Ephesians 4:4 teaches us about one church, one mission: "There is one body and one Spirit, just as you were called to one hope when you were called." Keep this unity goal in mind as you consider each God-led opportunity to serve.

Caution: After you've been serving for a while, it's easy to get so caught up in *serving, serving, serving* that you lose sight of the fact that your service is not for your own glory but for the glory and honor of God and the advancement of His kingdom. So continually ask yourself, "Why am I doing this?"

Step 5: Be open and trust God's LORDSHIP.

We each have skills that can be further developed, so you're not going to be the perfect teacher. You can, however, be perfect in your obedience to the Lord by not giving up. When helping others, keep in mind that you're going to make mistakes—and *that's okay!* The best teacher-student relationships come out of genuineness and vulnerability. You can be real—human! Here is an example of that: "Hey, I don't necessarily have this down yet but I'm doing my best and want to try to help you do better."

Side Note: The term *student* is not exclusive to those who are enrolled in school or are not yet adults; we are all students throughout life, and we each teach others in one way or another.

How am I pursuing vulnerability in my relationship with those I'm teaching?

_____

_____

How am I going to keep in mind what it was like for me to be taught by someone else? How can this help my approach to teaching others?

_____

_____

_____

_____

As a student (in any of my circumstances), what was the greatest learning experience I had? Why was it the greatest?

_____

_____

_____

_____

What would God say about my heart toward teaching others and receiving teaching?

_____

_____

_____

_____

What heart should I strive to have as a teacher and as a student?

_____

_____

_____

_____

Am I showing the right heart in my interactions? What is my spiritual posture?

_____

_____

_____

_____

_____

God will place on your heart or path people He wants you as a single person to help become better. Be humble and admit that you don't know or have all the answers and that you will always inquire of the Lord. Then make sure you practice what you preach: Commit yourself to always going to the Lord *first* for answers, seeking His direction through prayer and His Word. He will send people to help you accomplish His work and He will be so pleased that you stepped out in faith.

> Without faith it is impossible to please God.

> —Hebrews 11:6

Go to God for strength and wisdom! He will give you wisdom when you don't know what to do.

> If any of you lacks wisdom, you should ask God, who gives generously to all without finding fault, and it will be given to you.

> —James 1:5

CHAPTER EIGHT

Be Aware of Ladders

Breakups, Letdowns, Ending Up *Back* in the Pool

To maintain a healthy perspective throughout life, the biggest thing to keep in mind is that everything in life is only for a season. Nothing is guaranteed; nothing stays the same forever. All things are temporary—except for God, His Word, and eternity, which are everlasting. With this in mind, wouldn't you think the wisest one to put your complete hope in is Christ? This is important for me to share because once we develop an interest in someone and start dating, or even get married, we sometimes think, *Yay! I'm done! No more waiting! I found my godly mate! Nothing but happiness for the rest of my life! Happily ever after!*

No. Not at all.

With a "happily ever after" mind-set, our security becomes completely warped all over again, which is why marriage vows typically include "for better, for worse, for richer, for poorer, in sickness and in health, to love and to cherish till death do us part." While our wedding vows should remain permanent (till death do us part), nothing in life is permanent. There is no guarantee that anything will remain the same forever, even within the permanency of marriage, because death itself will eventually arrive. With this truth in mind, who would want to pursue or marry someone who is on their deathbed? Not trying to be morbid here, just drawing a point. Still with me? Good.

Typically, mutual interests and attractions begin when someone is in the prime of their life, which stereotypically looks like this: you look great (young), you're doing well spiritually and mentally, you have a decent job, and everything is awesome. Again, drawing out a point: the idea here is to begin marriage on the right foot. Right? Right. In other words, begin a marriage with the best possible advantages. Yet, in contrast to this perfect image and ideal circumstances, it's amazing to consider how much truer and permanent God's love is for us. "While we were still sinners, Christ died for us" (Romans 5:8). Jesus Christ chose to pursue and "marry" us while we were still on our spiritual deathbeds. We trust that our union to Him through faith and baptism will make us beautiful and radiant (that perfect image), so how much more grateful should we be for His sacrifice, knowing He died that we might choose to be with Him when, regardless of our choice, He was willing to die for us anyway?

When developing interests in others, shouldn't we have much more confidence in Jesus Christ as our one, true, indelible security and first union? Yes! Why then do the heartbroken within the kingdom of God so often end up leaving the church? Those who started dating within the kingdom and were let down. Those who have gone through breakups. Those who have had years and years of relationship disappointment. Those whose engagements fell through.

Are those who walk away from the church, and ultimately their faith, good examples of people who put their full hope, trust, and security in Christ? No. This is why it's so important for us to be aware of "ladders." *What . . . what ladders? Wait a second here. Let's talk more about this. What exactly is a ladder anyway? First, talk of pools, then floaties, and lifeguards, now ladders?* The answer is yes. I want to take this moment to address the importance of being cautious of these tricky things (ladders) that so often go unnoticed if not brought to the forefront of our attention. Take a moment to consider a swimming pool. You're standing at the shallow end and looking to the opposite end (deep water). What do you notice along the side? You guessed it. A ladder.

Pool ladders were designed as a safety feature. In the unfortunate event that someone experiences difficulty swimming in the deep end and does not have the energy or strength to make it to the safer end of the pool (shallow), they have an opportunity to swim to the ladder and get out of the pool. Genius safety feature, right? I agree. However, in our context, the ladder is *not* your friend when considering the pool as your singlehood. I will explain why.

First, ladders are our short-term relationships that we try to make permanent out of fear. While learning to swim in the life pool as a single, you may notice a ladder that seems like a safe escape route from the deep end. However, when you unknowingly practice a heart of discontentment, you risk using the ladder for the wrong purpose.

Remember my explanation that my ledges were empty relationships that were preventing me from learning how to swim and embrace my singleness. Hanging onto ledges kept me in the stage of immaturity much longer than desired. You can end up doing the same when you find yourself struggling in the deep end of life as a single. You may swim frantically toward the nearest escape (ladder) instead of persevering, overcoming your fears, and embracing your current stage of life.

Let me be clear. I am not saying that someone who is in danger and actually drowning or struggling for their life should not use the safety ladder. That's what it's there for! In that case, please, please use the ladder. What I am saying is to be mindful that there may be points in your life when you *feel* as though you have arrived at adulthood, you're embracing singleness, and fully content in the

Lord, only to realize you are not. This is what "ending up back in the pool" looks like.

Now consider a literal pool again and a person who does need the safety ladder. They were learning how to swim in the deep end, got tired, and hopped out by way of the ladder. This is perfectly okay and a good, a common practice, right? Right. Now, what if the person decided they no longer needed to practice swimming because they made it out just fine with the ladder, and they falsely believe they are a "good enough swimmer." What would you tell that person? I'm hoping the truth: "Get back into the water and continue learning how to swim!" Why? For the greater advantage of safety, security, and confidence as a swimmer—not only for their own sake but also for the sake of helping others learning to swim. This is exactly what I mean when advising that premarital relationships of less experienced swimmers in singlehood should end to give them the critical time needed to learn how to first swim *well* as a single. This gives them time to become well-equipped (expert swimmers and lifeguards) to survive the challenges and uncertainties of life (ocean). They still have much more they need to learn before committing to someone else.

As an expert swimmer now (enjoying singleness, owning adulthood, ultimately reaching maturity in Christ), you are skilled at being cautious to stay clear of your ladders and your ledges because you've come to know and understand your weaknesses. Perhaps you've even developed your strengths to the degree that you can serve as a lifeguard for those around you. If it so happens that you encounter a mutual interest that develops into a really great, healthy dating relationship, this circumstance is still no guarantee that God's plan for you in that relationship is marriage. I encourage you to keep an open mind that God's purpose for that particular relationship may be for you (or the other, or both) to further grow in emotional and spiritual maturity and skills through that season. Therefore, be sure to:

- Keep in mind that a dating experience is for a season. I encourage you to read Ecclesiastes 3, as it talks a great deal about seasons, what they look like, and the response we need to have. As for singles . . .

  > You who are young, be happy while you are young, and let your heart give you joy in the days of your youth. Follow the ways of your heart and whatever your eyes see, but know that for all these things God will bring you into judgment. So then, banish anxiety from your heart and cast off the troubles of your body, for youth and vigor are meaningless.
  >
  > —Ecclesiastes 11:9–10

- Pray for wisdom and have the maturity to understand that God does not waste a second of our time or any of our experiences and thereby does not waste our relationships (even within the kingdom) that do not lead to the altar of marriage.

  > A person's steps are directed by the Lord. How then can anyone understand their own way?
  >
  > —Proverbs 20:24

- Learn to trust that breakups are also for a *purpose* and God will use every relationship to teach you both something that could not have otherwise been learned, even when that relationship lasts for just a little while.

  > The wise prevail through great power, and those who have knowledge muster their strength. Surely you need guidance to wage war, and victory is won through many advisers.
  >
  > —Proverbs 24:5–6

Coming from someone who was twenty-three years old and had not yet dated, I understand that this concept is easier said than done. So, how about coming from someone a little older who recently experienced their first relationship that ended in a breakup after two and a half years?

Side Note: When I initially jotted down my thoughts for this book, I was around twenty-two years old. Although I felt that God had for years been putting the themes for this book on my heart, I was the classic definition of a *hot mess* and entirely too eager for a relationship. During the writing experience I discovered that there were definitely emotional aspects and feelings I couldn't relate to or even identify with at that time, such as breakups. Letdowns, though? Absolutely. I had been let down plenty of times by guys over the years—through crushes, interests, sparkles, internal butterflies, and the like. Even so, the only thing I was sure of at that time was that I had learned from the relationship experiences of my peers. I empathized with the heartaches they were going through over breakups and saw personally just how important it is to never let your guard down when it comes to placing your deepest hopes in another human being. Our deepest hopes belong to only one: Jesus Christ.

Thankfully, during my own time of singleness as I waited on God's timing to start dating in addition to learning from my peers, I learned to pray and fast for God's wisdom to identify seasonal relationships and how to be okay with those. When I considered what it could look like for me if I ended up "back in the pool" (meaning I needed to continue learning how to become a skilled swimmer), I realized I wasn't as ready for the ocean as I had thought I was. I envisioned starting my dating season and thinking, *I'm done with singlehood! The waiting is finally over!*

Honestly, my hope was to marry my first boyfriend, but would I truly be okay and content if that were not the case?

Remember the older person I mentioned previously who had recently experienced a breakup after two and a half years in her first relationship? Well, that person is me. That's another instance I'm choosing to be vague about at this time to avoid shifting from the purpose of this book. However, I will share that the experience tested every word I've written on the pages of this book. I've already addressed my preference and prioritization for transparency and can honestly say that my breakup experience was one of the hardest experiences of my life thus far. Definitely among my top five most difficult experiences.

I went through a period when I deeply struggled to read my Bible and pray, let alone write. My editors know, and I am grateful for their patience! Yet, I believe firmly that God was with me throughout the writing process, and I believe He allowed me to go through that pain not only for me to grow personally—including learning that I can survive by His grace—but also to share with you my authentic experiences and the victories of getting through those for the better—my emotional and spiritual growth. This is why it's important to ask yourself the following questions.

If you have not yet dated . . .

How can I *test* my contentment in the gray areas of my singleness?

If you have dated and have gone through a breakup or letdown . . .

How can I strive to be content in the gray areas of my singleness?

Walk with Me

Step 1: Whose side are you SWIMMING on?

Sometimes we forget that being single is a *blessing!*

> Our true and greatest purpose in life is found in our relationship with the forever lasting God, not in temporary man.

The way you might react to a breakup can be reflected by how your free time is spent.

Are most of my leisure time and thoughts about relationships or about spending time with the Lord, advancing God's kingdom, and looking for ways to serve?

_____

_____

_____

_____

_____

Chances are, your current focus will be your later focus as well. I encourage you to make sure your focus is always on how you can be the *best you* for God rather than on being the best spouse, parent, family member, friend, student, etc. These are important too, as long as they do not take priority over your focus on God and your love for Him.

Step 2: ENJOY the process!

Relationships are excellent tools to get different emotional muscles pumping! Just don't be discouraged if learning how to be in a relationship is the only thing you gain from that season.

- Be mindful of the positive aspects of dating.
- Exercise feelings of commitment.
- Learn how to be with another individual and identify as a couple or unit, which is an entirely different experience.

What are some benefits of my being in a God-centered relationship?

_____

_____

_____

What are some ways I can exercise feelings of commitment in other relationships in my life?

_____

_____

Are there any relationships (non-romantic) in my life that are lacking because of my failure to commit wholeheartedly? If so, what are they? Why are they lacking?

_____

_____

How can I be committed in a relationship and not place my identity in it?

_____

_____

How does God define wholeheartedness? (Hint: Mark 12:30)

_____

_____

Step 3: IDENTIFY the ladder and don't freak out.

The thrill of a relationship or the idea of being with your "dream" guy or girl can often be amped up by your friends, family members, and even your spiritual advisors.

> It is a trap to dedicate something rashly and only later to consider one's vows.
>
> —Proverbs 20:25

Don't be this person!

When the excitement starts to dwindle, give it to the Lord. Inquire of Him in prayer, "What am I supposed to be learning right now? Teach me and show me. Should I continue to hold on or let go?" Don't be afraid to ask the hard questions! Why hold onto something that was only supposed to be temporary anyway?

Am I placing my trust in God with this process or am I placing my trust in others?

_____

How can I continue to be honest about my desires without running ahead of God?

_____

_____

Did I consult with God before committing to this relationship?

_____

_____

> "I warned you when you felt secure, but you said, 'I will not listen!' This has been your way from your youth; you have not obeyed me."
>
> —Jeremiah 22:21

I identify a great deal with this verse. I encourage you not to make the same mistakes I did as a single. In the event you think, you think, you *may think* you're starting to develop romantic feelings for someone, ask God about it *first*. Please.

Step 4: LEARN all the more.

The single time in life is rich with opportunities to learn from God in new ways, so don't miss out on them!

- Take this time in your life to journal. Write to God all that you're learning.
- Be mindful of the ways He is using the other person in your life to express His love for you in what you're learning.
- Say thank you to those around you, for no reason—and often. You never know when you won't have the opportunity to do that anymore.

Step 5: Stay ALIVE!

When the excitement of a relationship has risen, common questions start to trickle in after a time: When are you going to get married? How many kids do you want? What kind of job do you have that will support you both? Where do you want to live? Do your families like each other?

Although these questions may come from a good place (prayerfully), don't be surprised when out of excitement people start to come for your entire life, asking questions that are *way* out of your season and thereby inappropriate. If this does happen to you, I encourage you to politely redirect the questions by simply responding with grace that you appreciate their care but need to guard your heart. Don't allow yourself to get entangled in the questions of others if those questions are causing you discontentment or a need to rush things along. Be concerned only about what God has specifically instructed you to do—and when to do it—in your romantic relationship.

In addition, when taking on such questions between the two of you, be sure you're allowing God to be in the driver's seat. Otherwise, you're both tempting a ticking clock—your own or someone else's agenda or timeline! As a couple, in God's time and at His pace, be encouraged by Ecclesiastes 3:11.

With the guidance of your accountability partners, I encourage you and the one you're dating to ask each other these questions:

Are we being patient?

_____

_____

Are we being God led or are we allowing others to influence our decisions?

_____

_____

Are we allowing our bodies to influence our decisions?

_____

_____

While growing as a couple, are we still truly God-focused and outwardly focused?

_____

_____

_____

To be completely honest, I've spent my fair amount of time as a single woman daydreaming about when "that special someone" would ask me out on that perfect date and start pursuing me, doing everything he could—going out of his way—to sweep me off my feet. Before I finally let the daydream go, I had to surrender my future and heart over to God. If I had not done that, those very thoughts may have forever been a daydream.

> Do not let your heart envy sinners, but always be zealous for the fear of the Lord. There is surely a future hope for you, and your hope will not be cut off.
>
> —Proverbs 23:17–18

CHAPTER NINE

Ready for the Stairs

Exiting Adolescent and Entering Adult Singleness

I have not yet dated but I believe God has nonetheless chosen me to share my thoughts. It is with great humility that I've come this far in my journey with the Lord, and I'm honored to share this portion of my book as a single woman. May it bring encouragement to all singles out there, as well as myself, once the Lord leads me to this chapter in my own life—someday.

At the time I wrote the above opening, I was in my early twenties and, to my dismay, my understanding of getting "out of the pool" was, admittedly, my desperate desire to be—you guessed it—in a relationship. I decided to retain that original opening to preserve the authenticity of my thoughts, feelings, and emotions from that stage in my life to help portray the full representation of my raw mind-set at that time.

As I continued to grow older, God made it abundantly clear to me that entering a relationship was *not* the way out of the pool. This fact led me to change the original chapter title from "Let's take the Stairs" (with the image and idea that two mature adults would be exiting the pool of singleness together) to "Ready for the Stairs." Being ready for the pool stairs is directly correlated with finally exiting adolescence and transitioning into adult singleness—the ocean.

Being an "infant in Christ" (1 Corinthians 3:1) can arguably be equated to literally swimming in a kiddie pool: Your parents are actively involved in your care because you cannot be left in the pool on your own and you are, in fact, single. This time in your life is, naturally, an acceptable time to be dependent on your parents or guardians. Once you grow older, from a child to a teen and then into young adulthood, and become acclimated to each new phase, you become a little more independent.

Being pursued is one of the most beautiful seasons of a person's life. There are simply no words for the wonder of knowing you are truly honored, valued, and adored by another human being. The purpose of beginning a relationship, especially in the kingdom, is that two people have grown fond of each other and want to continue getting to know each other, perhaps all the way to the altar and for the rest of their lives. However, for Christians, the purpose of being in a relationship is focused not only on this earthly life as a couple but also on the life to come: eternity. Partnering to prepare one another for eternity—devoting a portion of your life to helping your spouse get to heaven too—is now just as much a priority to you as getting yourself to heaven.

> Relationships that are focused on eternity from the very beginning are the ones that *thrive.*

They thrive because two eternity-focused individuals are coming together to *share* in the eternity focus and their undivided devotion to the Lord so they can accomplish more as a couple than they could as single individuals.

After what seemed to me like months of swimming, day in and day out (truly enjoying my singleness), I found myself becoming interested in one particular person I was growing fond of (my now-husband). Keeping my focus on *God's* future for me rather than thinking too far ahead into *our* future was a challenge. I learned right away that simply having an interest in someone and praying for a mutual interest wasn't enough to maintain my focus on God's best for me. I also found that I had to continue guarding my heart constantly and taking captive every thought regarding how I was feeling and what was actually going on: starting a new friendship with the opposite sex in the kingdom. Much like learning a new skill, it took a lot of practice to remain kingdom focused, which also included setting boundaries in my new-found relationship and sticking with those boundaries.

These are the essential steps we needed to take as our friendship and relationship grew:

- Seeking and applying advice from those who were older and wiser
- Inviting others into our lives to hold us accountable
- Holding ourselves accountable by being open and honest with each other

With time, we developed a sense of trust in each other—but that didn't happen overnight. I think this process of gradual growth is generally different for guys and girls, outside the obvious physical attraction they may have. Typically, girls tend to grow attached early on whereas guys tend to need time to see, and even understand, how they're feeling toward their interest before the relationship develops into something more.

As I shared in the chapter opening, I had not entered into a romantic relationship before. In real time, my budding relationship with the brother in the kingdom was a new (and even nerve-wracking) experience for me. I'm excited to share these very real feelings and details of our process with you because that experience taught me how to grow in my faith, trust God with all my being, and pursue my fullest potential in my walk with Him, while still being willing to yield to His will over mine. This was done only by trusting that He knew best and knew me better than I knew myself because He created me. Crazy lessons to learn, right? Yet learning these very things have been the most rewarding parts of my journey with Christ over the past thirteen years.

Remember at the beginning of the book when I shared that God had asked me, "Why are you choosing to stay in the pool when I'm preparing you for the ocean?" At that time in my life I was confused because I honestly thought I was trusting God and His timing—something I had grown accustomed to *saying* while growing up. It wasn't until my college days that the Lord revealed to me that my *actions* (thereby my heart) were not reflecting my understanding of what it truly means to trust God and His timing. My outward actions were exemplifying what was really going on in the deepest parts of my heart: my desire to live life taking matters into my own hands, being my own lord, trusting in my own self, and doing things in my own timing.

> Though I constantly take my life in my own hands, I
> will not forget your law.
>
> —Psalm 119:109

As I continued my walk with God, I felt as though He would not allow me to forget His law. I felt the Lord's protection consistently as the events of my life continued to unfold over time. Yet for a long while before I had this change of heart, instead of allowing myself to mature as a young woman, I grew comfortable holding onto temporary, unhealthy, fake relationships instead of learning how to enjoy being single. Now I'm happy to confidently proclaim that I eventually truly became happy as a *single woman of God!*

To be honest, I was also a little fearful of all the responsibility that comes with the life I desired to have someday as a girlfriend, prayerfully a wife, and hopefully a mom. But I had grown to *trust* that God would *prepare* me for those upcoming stages in my life rather than throw a boyfriend, husband, and children at me and expect me to know what to do with them. In dating, God didn't just throw a boyfriend at me and say, "Here!" He blessed me with a true friend, a friendship, and He let me decide what I wanted to do with that friendship . . . how I would treat that brother . . . and what I was willing to see God do with that relationship. Even now, I constantly remind myself that our friendship belongs to God, meaning it is God's friendship too, not simply our own. Weird way to phrase it, right? I feel this is an accurate description because if we keep the concept in mind that the friendship with our romantic interest belongs to God first and foremost, that attitude will directly and positively impact how we interact with each other *within* the friendship.

When a friendship is being led toward a romantic relationship, this is an exciting time, right? Embarking on this transformation into something deeper and greater (much like learning how to swim) the couple must have the time and boundaries needed to learn how best to walk together with Christ in the center—that three-strand cord that's not easily broken (Ecclesiastes 4:12).

Walking with Christ as a single is also a relationship process that mandates the investment of a lot of time and commitment—and that friendship (John 15:15) is so enjoyable! My prayer is that our human partnering relationships are equally rewarding.

Now I want to take a moment to pause here because, again, I want to make it abundantly clear that the *goal*—the way out of the pool—is not to enter into a relationship. God's lesson behind placing us in a pool of singleness is so we can learn how to build the techniques and strength we need to overcome the greater trials and hurdles that will come later in adulthood.

Embracing singleness and learning how to swim takes many different forms and timelines for everyone. I entered into a relationship around the same time that my season of spiritual adolescence ended and I was embracing my adulthood in Christ.

I'm not implying that following this same timeline will lead you down the exact path as mine, not at all. Everyone's life is different, and God has an equally special and unique plan for each individual. For example, I think about the amazing single mothers out there who have learned a great deal about life, are responsible for the lives of their children, and have managed to mature and embrace adulthood in ways I cannot begin to imagine because I am not a mom. And I consider the single fathers who have also made tough life decisions at a young age. Their entrance into adulthood may have started earlier than expected. I also think of those who lost a parent or another significant person at a young age and had to grow up overnight to some extent. The unique journeys of others are countless and endless.

I urge you to envision yourself inside your pool of life and consider what exiting this stage might look like *for you.* For me, I chose to specifically address the area of my discontentment as a single adult because that was my unique journey. My prayer is that my shared experience and knowledge will be a help to you.

Ladies . . .

Keep in mind that the *man* inherently, instinctively needs to lead the relationship because this is God's plan and design for key reasons. I could write a whole other book on this subject, but for now learn about this from the source: God's Word. Trust Him that relationships work better when we obey God and allow the guy in our life to lead the way at the pace God wants to lead him and our relationship. The reason this truth needs to be talked about, learned early on, and accepted (by both women and men) is that this is God's plan, explained in Genesis 2:22–24.

> The Lord God made a woman from the rib he had taken out of the man, and he brought her to the man. The man said, "This is now bone of my bones and flesh of my flesh; she shall be called 'woman,' for she was taken out of man." That is why a man leaves his father

and mother and is united to his wife, and they become one flesh.

The man leading is not just a cultural expectation—it's a command of God.

One of my favorite parts of my own romantic friendship is the focus that we're set apart from the world. I grew up going to church, so I've always felt set apart, but the way I was used to thinking while interacting with the opposite sex was definitely not set apart. I am not saying this is where we were in our friendship at the time; however, I could see why it's important to be mindful and intentional when starting and maintaining a friendship with the opposite sex. The lack of distinguished goals and mutually agreed on understandings leads to sin and ultimately turns the relationship completely *away* from God.

Starting to get the idea here? Good. I'm glad.

The grand decision that a man makes to commit to a woman— both great swimmers, owning their singleness and enjoying it wholeheartedly—to lead her through the challenges in their lives is what I like to call entering "courtship." This means committing to a long, formal process of learning how to walk together (swim side by side together with God) in pursuit of righteousness toward swimming with Christ as the center of the relationship. This can take place while the two are still in the pool (individually and as a couple practicing their walk with Christ together) or already in the ocean (in a deeper walk together with Christ).

Courtship is shaped in accordance with God's timing and the stage of life you're currently in. Once you arrive at the ocean, you've already obtained the concept of swimming as an expert. There are significant differences between swimming in a pool and swimming in the ocean:

- In the pool, the conditions are consistent; you have lifeguards on hand to help you and the comfort that other people are learning alongside you.
- In the ocean, the conditions are far more complex: the depth, seaweed, sand, creatures, waves, undercurrents, storms, and other unexpected conditions you could encounter at any given moment.

The point is to take time to become an expert swimmer in a pool before swimming in the ocean. Is the whole concept of swimming as related to embracing singleness and obtaining maturity making more sense now? I hope so. In the following Walk with Me section, I address what being "ready for the stairs" looks like for those who are entering a relationship or courtship and for those who are not in a relationship.

For those who would like to date in the near future, consider the relationship or romantic *interest* you may currently have and how you're feeling in general as you approach the closing pages of this book.

While reading this book, has my attitude toward God, my singleness, and adulthood changed? Why or why not?

_____

_____

_____

_____

_____

_____

If I'm still holding onto something, unwilling to let go to start fully enjoying reaching spiritual and emotional adulthood in relationship with God and embracing singleness, why is that? What's holding me back?

_____

_____

_____

_____

_____

For those in a courting relationship: Does my current relationship reflect an eternity focus or a selfish inward focus?

_____

_____

Are we both expressing healthy boundaries and have we both developed a sense of trust and safety with each other that is pure and righteous? Or have we both confided in each other instead of going to God together? Have we committed secret sin together that we've agreed to not confess to God or share with our lifeguards?

_____

_____

_____

_____

_____

_____

To be entirely honest, there was a time when I was on the other side of this story. I was the sister still holding on to and obsessing over my ledges instead of just trusting God and being completely willing to learn everything He planned to teach me. There were times, even in my great romantic friendship I finally had, that I found myself longing for my fondest ledges for various reasons, so I understand it's not easy to let go. Such times will come in your life, but you must persevere to push through and allow yourself to understand that these experiences are nothing more than *memories*. More importantly, these experiences are *lessons*.

If God wanted a relationship of your past to be part of your present life, it would be, and He would have made that abundantly clear to you. So I encourage you to let go of past ledges right now, whatever those may be. As I shared early in the book, my ledges were the guys I clung to. In your heart, just let go of those because God has you secure in His almighty hands! Because of His great love and faithfulness as your heavenly Father and provider, you will be fine. Trust Him.

If you've learned and are practicing the swim lessons shared in this book, you can swim now! Congratulations! And if you haven't yet approached the ocean, someday you'll enjoy swimming in a beautiful ocean journey as a strong adult in Christ—maybe with the mate God has planned for you or maybe without. Just trust Him.

> In all your ways submit to him, and he will make your
> paths straight.
>
> —Proverbs 3:6

How do you know if you're ready for the stairs?

Walk with Me

For those entering or already in a relationship.

Step 1: Develop an AWESOME friendship.

It's easy to get caught up in the idea of wanting to be in a relationship and easy to become distracted by physical attraction even though we're not yet close to the person. Do not allow for your goal to be a physical closeness to them. This is a direct warning.

What are the conversations between my interest and me typically centered on?

_____

_____

_____

_____

Can I honestly say there's a friendship being built with Christ as the center?

_____

_____

_____

Men . . .

Am I allowing God to work through me in leading my friendship by initiating the courtship?

_____

_____

_____

Women . . .

Am I always the one initiating or is there a mutual amount of effort taking place in the friendship?

_____

_____

_____

Couple:

Are we playing games (mind games perhaps), or is there a mutual respect between the two of us?

_____

_____

_____

Step 2: Keep up with the CONTENTMENT.

Of course, it's an exciting time when you're noticed by someone or your interest in someone starts to be reciprocated, but don't allow future hopes and expectations to prevent you from enjoying the *process* of learning and growing with each another in the meantime.

Together, make a list of necessary boundaries to be implemented to sustain a healthy friendship and potential relationship. Write your agreed upon list here.

_____

_____

_____

_____

_____

_____

Are we okay with and grateful for the boundaries we have developed? Why or why not?

_____

_____

_____

_____

Do we see why boundaries are necessary? And are we going out of our way to protect those boundaries? How?

_____

_____

_____

Do we look for ways to bend the rules "just this once" or are we open (with our accountability partners) about our temptations before causing the other person in the relationship to stumble?

_____

_____

_____

Is our friendship completely in the light or are there hidden things we're both aware of but have decided not to talk about, instead just letting those conversations go and promising "we will not do it again"? If so, why? How will we go about confronting our hidden sin?

_____

_____

_____

_____

_____

Step 3: Letting the MAN lead the way.

Ladies and gentlemen, a *great* way to know if your relationship is healthy and from the Lord is by determining if the *man* is the one navigating from the beginning and moving forward.

Men . . .

Have I prayed about the romantic friendship? Am I consistently asking God what to do in terms of pursuing this courtship?

_____

Am I seeking advice from my lifeguard?

_____

Am I being consistent in my relationship with God and the one I'm pursuing?

_____

Women . . .

Am I praying about the romantic friendship? Am I consistently inquiring of God and allowing the man of God to *lead* me, or have I decided to take matters into my own hands and manipulate in small or large ways? (Be honest.)

_____

_____

_____

_____

_____

_____

If I'm taking matters into my own hands, what do I need to do, beginning right now, to change in order for our courtship to look like God's plan?

_____

_____

_____

You don't have to end the friendship altogether, but definitely consider taking a few steps back for a little while to regain (or gain) the footing God intended for you as a woman of God.

Step 4: Is he or she WORTH the wait?

Sometimes, for whatever reason, once we finally have a friendship with our romantic interest and discover it's mutual, we may start to think to ourselves, "Man, I can do better." We, both men and women, can become so worldly and *prideful*.

Is this my mind-set or do I value and appreciate the romantic friendship so much that I'll do whatever it takes to protect it? And do I genuinely want to help my friend get to heaven as much as they want to help me?

_____

_____

_____

_____

> Individuals who think in worldly ways do not have relationships that are eternity focused.

Pray for each other if you're not yet doing so. You both will benefit from reevaluating; consider including more joint time with God in your friendship.

How are we both making God number one in our relationship?

_____

_____

_____

Are we both authentically eternity focused, praying for each other, and taking action that indicates that Christ and eternity are the focuses in our relationship?

_____

_____

Step 5: Don't be afraid to let your LIGHT SHINE!

In developing a friendship or romantic interest within the kingdom, there can unfortunately be a fear regarding talking with each other about God (at least at first) because you fear you may come across to each other as wanting to impress or as "too spiritual." Let go of this myth and shine on!

Do we lift each other up when there are successes? How?

_____

_____

_____

Do we call each other out with love when there are failures? Give an example.

_____

_____

_____

_____

These are the practicing components that lead to a healthy relationship.

> Relationships that never go through any challenges and trials can never grow.

Are we collectively shining for God or are we too into ourselves to have time for anything else?

_____

_____

If your friendship is too self-focused.

What can we do within ourselves and as a couple to change this, beginning today?

_____

_____

_____

If you're collectively shining for God:

What can we do within ourselves and as a couple to enhance our collective strengths?

_____

_____

_____

_____

> Daughters of Jerusalem, I charge you by the gazelles and by the does of the field: Do not arouse or awaken love until it so desires.
>
> —Song of Songs 2:7

Let God do His thing in His timing. And men, be bold and courageous, trusting that the Lord is on your side. Couples: ENJOY!

For those not in a relationship.

Step 1: Deepen your friendship with God.

> I no longer call you servants, because a servant does not know his master's business. Instead, I have called you friends, for everything that I learned from my Father I have made known to you.

—John 15:15

How would I describe the current state of my relationship with God?

_____

_____

Would I categorize my relationship with God as a friendship? Why or why not?

_____

_____

Step 2: Keep up with the CONTENTMENT.

> I am not saying this because I am in need, for I have learned to be content whatever the circumstances. I know what it is to be in need, and I know what it is to have plenty. I have learned the secret of being content in any and every situation, whether well fed or hungry, whether living in plenty or in want. I can do all this through him who gives me strength.

—Philippians 4:11–13

Meditating on this verse, I believe these are the ways I can grow in being content in all circumstances.

_____

_____

_____

_____

What would living out this verse look like for me?

_____

_____

_____

_____

Step 3: Letting GOD lead the way.

> Whether you turn to the right or to the left, your ears will hear a voice behind you, saying, "This is the way; walk in it."

—Isaiah 30:21

Am I listening to God's voice?

_____

_____

What scriptures are guiding me and influencing my daily life decisions?

_____

_____

_____

_____

How well have I been following my list of scriptures?

_____

_____

What enables me to follow them? What prevents me from following them?

_____

_____

_____

_____

Step 4: Are your desires worth the WAIT?

> Take delight in the LORD, and he will give you the desires of your heart.
>
> —Psalm 37:4

Am I enjoying the journey and allowing God to direct the way?

_____

Am I still sharing with God my deepest desires? Or am I hiding them out of fear of letting them go?

_____

_____

Step 5: Don't be afraid to let your light SHINE.

> For this reason I remind you to fan into flame the gift of God, which is in you through the laying on of my hands. For the Spirit God gave us does not make us timid, but gives us power, love and self-discipline.
>
> —2 Timothy 1:6–7

| Be fearless as you enjoy your singleness and embrace your adulthood in Christ! |

Am I too shy to share with others all the ways God has been working in my life? If so, why?

_____

_____

_____

_____

_____

Who can I share with today about how much God has proven Himself faithful in my singleness? What can I share?

_____

_____

_____

_____

Why is sharing my spiritual journey with those around me important?

_____

_____

_____

How can sharing with others be helpful to me?

_____

_____

_____

Since we are surrounded by such a great cloud of witnesses, let us throw off everything that hinders and the sin that so easily entangles. And let us run with perseverance the race marked out for us.

—Hebrews 12:1

CHAPTER TEN

I've Been Swimming for Years. Now What?

Longtime Swimmers

As more time passes, the harder it can become to be patient and wait on God. Doubt definitely started to creep into me after a while, especially as I approached graduating from college and starting my career. But trust me when I say this: God's timing is perfect. You have to *believe* He knows exactly what He's doing, He is fully aware of your needs, and He is a God who wants you to find your joy in Him and wants to tend to your desires as well. Let your faith shine!

Developing a skill is one thing, but mastering it is another. I hope by reading this book you're starting to feel your skills develop in accepting, embracing, owning, and *enjoying* your

singlehood. And I hope you're now basking in the joy of this season of your life, gifted to you by God to enhance those skills and allow them to grow.

Older singles, I understand you may feel some forms of discouragement while still in the waiting and may even be asking, "Well, what if I've been single *forever*? I've been swimming for a while, I truly believe I'm content, and still nothing is showing promise that my current stage in life will move toward a relationship." I'm going to be completely honest with you and encourage you to commit to participating in two specific spiritual practices: pray and fast.

Decide today to go on a fast and specifically pray to feel close to God in this particular area of your life. The worst thing Satan can do when you feel as if you've been waiting patiently for something or someone is to plant in you the lie that God doesn't care or has completely forgotten about you. Those are lies. Counter his attack with truth: God has not forgotten you! The other truth is that it's up to you to show Satan that you have not forgotten about him and are well prepared to battle against his schemes by daily putting on the armor of God! (See Ephesians 6:10–18.)

I understand that sometimes full submission of our lives and hearts to God is not easy, but as followers of Christ we are *all* called to submit to His authority. He already knows when we're not practicing true submission to Him, even when our actions say otherwise, because He is all-knowing, fully aware of what's going on in our hearts even when we don't. This is why David the palmist wrote this in his own prayer to God:

> Search me, God, and know my heart; test me and know
> my anxious thoughts. See if there is any offensive way in
> me, and lead me in the way everlasting.
>
> —Psalm 139:23–24

Ask yourself this:

What am I doing right now with my life?

And no, I'm not encouraging you to go out and start participating in a bunch of *works* for God. I'm asking you to really question yourself: What am I doing right now with my life?

_____

_____

_____

Am I living for God or living for myself?

_____

Do I have focused goals outside of getting into a relationship?

_____

_____

Do I feel as though my life will not *really* start until I'm in a relationship?

I encourage you to ask yourself what direction your life is headed and write out your honest answer here.

_____

_____

_____

_____

_____

Am I allowing fear to prevent me from moving forward because I don't know what I would want my next step to be, other than a relationship? Why is that?

_____

_____

_____

_____

_____

> You'd be surprised by how much God has in store for you already! He's just waiting for you to be on board with Him!

Maybe you're truly comfortable and content being single—amen if you are!—but God is asking you to be even more than content by not only accepting your singleness but also going out and *doing something* with it!

> What do workers gain from their toil? I have seen the burden God has laid on the human race. He has made everything beautiful in its time. He has also set eternity in the human heart; yet no one can fathom what God has done from beginning to end. I know that there is nothing better for people than to be happy and to do good while they live. That each of them may eat and drink, and find satisfaction in all their toil—this is the gift of God. I know that everything God does will endure forever; nothing can be added to it and nothing taken from it. God does it so that people will fear him.
>
> —Ecclesiastes 3:9–14

Truthfully, it's best to take time now, as a child of God, to express this to Him: "Father, I'm trying." If you don't, He—as your Holy Father who wholly loves you and wants to protect you—will have you submit to Him one way or another, as any truly loving and protective parent would. And as you've likely experienced under your earthly parent or guardian, "one way or another" is not usually the easiest or most enjoyable.

Once you've written your open and honest prayer to God, I encourage you to consider these questions:

- How will you live out the reality that your life is not your own?
- What does it mean for your life to *belong* to Christ?

When considering these issues, whether or not you're living life for God or yourself, keep in mind that *living for God* does not mean you'll never again do something you enjoy. That's one of Satan's greatest lies! In truth, God has given each of us gifts to pursue and use in our lives for His glory, His body (the Church), and the advancement of His kingdom that will give us great enjoyment and fulfilment.

> Just as each of us has one body with many members, and these members do not all have the same function, so in Christ we, though many, form one body, and each member belongs to all the others. We have different gifts, according to the grace given to each of us. If your gift is prophesying, then prophesy in accordance with your faith; if it is serving, then serve; if it is teaching, then teach; if it is to encourage, then give encouragement; if it is giving, then give generously; if it is to lead, do it diligently; if it is to show mercy, do it cheerfully.

—Romans 12:4–8

Walk with Me

Step 1: What are my GIFTS?

We learn by proactively doing. If you've served in a number of ways in an effort to discover your gifts, and your efforts didn't seem to work, don't sell yourself short. Continue to serve in areas that are new to you. As I said earlier, God doesn't waste a second of our time or experiences. When you try a number of different ministry tasks, God will not only strengthen the gifts you may not have yet discovered but will also use those new experiences to further sharpen your focus. Just as He will teach you things during short-lived relationships, He will also use your service experiences to show you more clearly which gifts are yours and which are not.

What is your enjoyable toil and what do you like doing?

_____

_____

_____

Think about that one thing that comes to mind when you picture yourself genuinely enjoying service for God.

What comes to my mind?

_____

_____

Maybe you haven't yet been proactive to step into that service.

What's keeping me from experiencing this task? Or if I have started the task and stopped, what caused that?

Side Note: Sometimes we can make excuses for not serving. I can specifically relate to this with various excuses: "God, I have work. I have school. My family is difficult and that's all I can manage. I'm a single parent. I'm a caretaker for my elderly parent. I don't have enough of . . ."

Please don't allow external stressors to prevent you from fulfilling other areas of your godly purpose.

Step 2: What am I to DO?

First, here's what *not* to do: Don't look to what others are doing as "the thing" you may think *you* should be doing. You are not another person and never will be. What God has purposed for others is not necessarily what He's purposed for *you* in your uniqueness. Pray for God to give you specific instructions. Even if you discover you have the same gift as someone else, you two are still different individuals who will complete tasks differently, as God sees fit. Be excited about that!

Do I struggle with the temptation to compare myself with others in the area of identifying my gifts?

Have I stopped further developing my gifts? If so, why?

_____

_____

Step 3: Be not afraid to FEAR Him.

Once you get started on your ministry task, keep in mind that the ultimate goal is to please God rather than trying to prove something to Him in hope that He'll reward you with what you want "in return." You cannot earn new seasons or different events in your life by doing things for God. He refers to such works as "filthy rags" (Isaiah 64:6) and He "judges the thoughts and attitudes of the heart" (Hebrews 4:12). Your acts of service should always come from your heart of desiring to worship, honor, obey, and fear your heavenly Father. With these scriptures in mind, ask yourself these questions:

Do I fear God? Truly and deeply? (Hint: not in a frightened sense, terrified, and completely afraid to talk to Him, but in *reverent understanding* of who He is and your place before Him.)

_____

_____

Am I completely surrendered in *reverence* to God with my entire life and whole heart?

_____

_____

How do my actions show that I fear and revere God?

_____

_____

If for whatever reason your answer is no, I urge you to take time to write an honest prayer asking God for forgiveness and inviting Him to search your heart and reveal to you what happened in your life that is preventing you from fearing Him in this healthy, reverent way.

Lord, I pray for the will to change my heart toward You by . . .

_____

_____

_____

You will know—just as He knows—if your heart in serving Him is genuinely out of your love for Him or aimed at a reward system of your own design. We cannot manipulate God, no matter how hard we try, but we can know that He's the giver of good gifts simply because He loves us so much.

Step 4: Remember, it's still NOT about you!

Reverence, as I've shared, is key in how we approach the Lord and how we think of Him.

Am I being humble right now or am I trying to demand things of God?

_____

What are my intentions behind praying this prayer?

_____

Do my prayers reflect that of an outward focus? Or inward focus?

_____

Side Note: Think back to the concept of treating God like Santa Claus. We do not want to practice this mentality or behavior within our hearts.

Step 5: Keep your faith ALIVE.

Remember 1 Peter 5:8: "Be alert and of sober mind. Your enemy the devil prowls around like a roaring lion looking for someone to devour." Satan *is* going to try to attack you—maybe not every day but every chance he gets. It's your responsibility to make sure those attacks are few because you are remaining on guard and using the armor of God and other tactics He has provided you in His Word. When you are attacked, be open about it with your lifeguards and all other wise counsel.

Who can I go to at any time and without shame to confess my sins?

_____

> Be alert and of sober mind. Your enemy the devil prowls around like a roaring lion looking for someone to devour. Resist him, standing firm in the faith, because you know that the family of believers throughout the world is undergoing the same kind of sufferings.
>
> —1 Peter 5:8–9

Allow my paraphrase if you will:

> Pay *attention* and don't lose *hope*. Your enemy the devil prowls around like a roaring lion looking for someone to *trap*. Refrain from being *caught*! Have conviction behind your faith because you know that this pool (or ocean) of swimmers—of all ages, races, life stages, backgrounds, and cultures—may be undergoing similar struggles in being content while single.

I know this may be a lot to take in. After completing this final chapter, you may still be asking yourself, "Where do I see myself now spiritually? Am I single in the pool?" (Am I embracing singleness, still with some important life lessons to learn before achieving full adulthood in Christ.) "Or am I single in the ocean?" (My adulthood in Christ has been achieved but I have not yet fully embraced singleness.)

Regardless of where you find yourself as you reach the closing pages of this book, always keep in mind that no matter what, "The one who calls you is faithful, and *he* will do it" (1 Thessalonians 5:24, author emphasis). As followers of Christ, we must learn to wait and rely on God while remembering the ultimate reward to obeying His commands is spending eternity with Him.

I would like to invite you into this grand opportunity, while developing your new swimming skills, to further emulate Christ's character by practicing His humility.

As the apostle Paul wrote in Philippians 2:1–10,

> Therefore if you have any encouragement from being united with Christ, if any comfort from his love, if any common sharing in the Spirit, if any tenderness and compassion, then make my joy complete by being like-minded, having the same love, being one in spirit

and of one mind. Do nothing out of selfish ambition or vain conceit. Rather, in humility value others above yourselves, not looking to your own interests but each of you to the interests of the others.

In your relationships with one another, have the same mindset as Christ Jesus: Who, being in very nature God, did not consider equality with God something to be used to his own advantage; rather, he made himself nothing by taking the very nature of a servant, being made in human likeness.

And being found in appearance as a man, he humbled himself by becoming obedient to death— even death on a cross! Therefore God exalted him to the highest place and gave him the name that is above every name, that at the name of Jesus every knee should bow, in heaven and on earth and under the earth.

So, my dear friend, I encourage you to be *excited* about being a living sacrifice for God and being obedient, even if that means being obedient to life on this earth as a single. Rather than adopting an attitude of fear based on what the past few years may have been, decide to change your heart and mind today. Realize there is so much more to your life as a single as you choose to live wholeheartedly for Christ. Trust that all your greatest and deepest desires *can* be fulfilled by a relationship if it is the right relationship, the one with our heavenly Father. Amen!

Journey Onward: Off to the Ocean

Many years later, out of the pool,
and finally swimming in the ocean.

~

A peek into the upcoming sequel, *Gone Sailing* . . .

As rain droplets began to create a small pool on the back of my Bible, I looked to my right and saw the waves in the canal along the edge of our apartment complex, crashing and lapping onto the shore near the deck. A storm was coming. Then I heard the Holy Spirit whisper, "Have I not already taught you how to survive in the ocean? Don't doubt; *just swim!*"

Newly married, my husband and I had just gotten into our first "real fight" as a married couple. You know the one, where suddenly you're not just play-fighting anymore but real-fighting, and what seemed like a small disagreement turned into an actual argument. Yeah, that's the one.

That was some time ago, so I honestly can't remember what the fight was about. My husband would tell you the same as he doesn't remember either. What I do remember is that we had been home from our honeymoon for about two weeks and were still adjusting to living together, having new work schedules, and combining daily routines as a married couple—and something just snapped between us.

Approaching the early stage of marriage, I had paused some life activities in order to really focus on my spouse. After seeking much advice, we agreed on doing a handful of things to support a prayerfully smooth transition into married life. We even *willingly* participated in what some would say are extreme or radical fasts, such as absolutely no social media for nearly a year. I know, gnarly, right? Just kidding. Yet for us (mostly me) it was a pretty big deal, one of the many decisions we made right before getting married. Even so, while participating in these various efforts to focus on becoming one, I could not believe I had stormed out of our newly furnished apartment because of an argument. There I sat with the tumultuous sea mimicking the turmoil inside me, thinking that all hope was already lost.

Now to be clear, I had not entered into marriage thinking that our relationship would consist of only blue skies and rainbows every day. No, not at all. But what I did not expect was to feel that level of defeat so early into our union.

For those of you who have read *Gone Swimming*, I hope you are already reaping the benefits of enjoying the Lord's instructions and thoroughly relishing your adult life in Christ and embracing your singleness, whether in the pool or the ocean. *Gone Sailing* is going to be quite different. This sequel shares what it's like not only to swim and sail in the ocean but also to live with a spouse as a newly married couple. Throughout this book, I'll share intimate details of our dating relationship and introduce to you for the first time the man who is very special and important to me, my husband, Ricardo Metayer. His voice will contribute the much needed male perspective.

Hello, everyone. Husband here! I will be providing the perspective of a once single man, now suddenly bearing the full weight of juggling thoughts, feelings, and dreams of two people as a committed spouse. A man who no longer interacts with my loving mother as the primary female influencer in my life.

Upon getting married, it quickly became evident that, in my current state, I was not enough to be the husband God called me to be. I had to start assessing my knowledge and convictions more thoroughly to find those that would better suit my new role. I had to become a stronger swimmer. When Tat first shared *Gone Swimming* with me, we were still dating. Having been a single man in the faith for a whole three years, I felt as though I had relevant insight worth sharing. But, as you can imagine, my influence at that time would have been inappropriate, given our not-yet-married relationship status. Now, a little older, much wiser, and *married,* I'm both honored and thrilled to be able to share the male perspective in *Gone Sailing.*

We hope you enjoy our collaborative efforts!

Gone Sailing . . .

Earlier, when I had fumed out of our apartment, it was clear as day. Once I'd taken a seat at our community pool (interestingly enough), it began to rain heavily. As I looked across the distance , that's when I saw it—a little black spot slowly but surely approached through the downpour. That little black spot gradually grew to a medium black spot and then to what I recognized as a black umbrella. Only a few moments later, I realized that underneath the umbrella was my husband. . . .

www.ingramcontent.com/pod-product-compliance
Lightning Source LLC
Chambersburg PA
CBHW030935090426
42737CB00007B/434